Meal of Mystery, Meal of Wonder

Malcolm Smith

TWS Publishing

Published in the United States of America

Paperback: ISBN 978-1-961180-73-4

TWS Publishing
Legacy Society Publishing, Inc.
Lodi, CA
www.thewriterssociety.online

LEGACY SOCIETY

Dedicated to Cheryl Young Smith

The one who holds the first place in stirring and encouraging me in the writing of this book is my wife. We were married in February 2021. She had not been married for 35 years, having spent that time working in women's jails and prisons—ten years as the Women's Staff Chaplain at Harris County Jail in Houston, Texas, the third-largest jail in the nation at that time.

I had been recently widowed, and we met during a weekend conference at her church, where I shared the love of God from the story of the Prodigal Son.

Marriage was not on either of our minds. We began as friends, sharing with each other the love of God in the Spirit. Our months of friendship developed through hours of talking and sharing our lives. We met in January 2020, just as COVID had taken hold and large gatherings were forbidden. I was grounded, and the invitations to speak were 'zero' after a year of bookings were canceled.

We had lunch at Landry's in Galveston, and as we left the restaurant, we paused outside, face to face, and made a covenant of friendship. Months later —during the Thanksgiving and Christmas holidays—I asked her to marry me. We married at a beautiful farmhouse in the country outside Katy/Fulshear, Texas on February 27, 2021.

We began ministering together as one voice. I began writing again, and this book on the Eucharist began to take shape. A short time after I committed to writing the book, I was diagnosed with lung cancer, melanoma, stage 4. Cheryl never left my side, sleeping on a cot in the corner of my hospital room. Writing was reduced to a few notes between days of inactivity. Some days were very dark as the medication affected me. During that time, the one stable person who kept me looking to Jesus was Cheryl. Sitting by my bed, she held me and spoke with the authority of the Holy Spirit, sharing a vision: "Step into the Ring of Life and DO NOT BOW TO YOUR OPPONENT. BOW ONLY UNTO ME. DO NOT BOW TO FEAR." *The Holy Spirit assured me that I would be out of the hospital and the book would be written.*

When I was released from the hospital, she continued to be my help meet, strengthening me to return to writing the book. The first chapters began to take shape. We sat on the porch, talked, asked questions, and the Holy Spirit led us to answers, which brought great joy in revelation.

Cheryl had very little background in church. Her only association was confirmation as a teen in the Lutheran Church. When confirmed, she could wear hose and shave her legs—a sign of growing up in a small town. But after coming to Christ in 1983 and plunging into prison ministry, she carried communion wherever she went and kept it by her bedside at home. My first gift to her, early in our friendship, was a gold-plated traveling communion set.

As I wrote the chapters, she spent long hours praying for me. When a chapter was completed in a first draft, she read and reread it, correcting grammar and editing. The chapters became the grounds for our discussions on our porch. Her questions led to my answers, which led us to more questions. Parts of this book would never have been written but for those conversations.

We are normally up by six in the morning, but there were times—with cups of coffee—that we were up at five, and one morning at four, to get to the heart of some truth. The manuscript was written and rewritten many times, reflecting those conversations.

I had not considered it before, but marriage is much like the Eucharist. It is a mystery and a wonder. In the hours spent writing this book, the mystery of two persons celebrating union without losing themselves in one another—and the wonder of joy in the union—was an ever-present reality. Cheryl increasingly found expression in the Eucharist every Sunday at our fellowship, and I felt the strength of knowing in depth what I had spent my life laying hold of.

On Wednesday, September 25, 2024, I was typing the last sentence of the last chapter when Cheryl burst into my study. The previous Tuesday, I had a PET scan, which scans my whole body for cancer. She had the results! She exclaimed that I was 100% cancer-free!

We sat on the porch that evening and celebrated: I was cancer-free, and the book was complete to the last sentence. We laughed—this was our Isaac, born of two old people. May it, like Isaac, set the world to laughing His laughter!

Acknowledgments

It is difficult to acknowledge all who have been part of this book. The journey began when I was in my teens, with no thought of writing a book—this one or any other! I will likely leave out some who left a deep impression on me at the time, but I still carry the understanding you planted in me. You have become part of the vast number of people who have left their imprint on my life over the last 70 years!

In no particular order, I must thank **Robin Smit**, my publisher. I have dealt with many publishers and editors over the decades, but Robin, you have given of yourself to make this book happen like no other! For your friendship to both my wife, Cheryl, in writing her book *To Love Again*, and for all my previous publications with The Writer's Society—I say with all my heart, "Thank you!" This book would never have been accomplished without you and your staff.

To **Gail Riley**, who works in our office in Bandera, and who is also my 'go-to' editor whenever I face questions in writing that leave me confused!

Dr. Alan Hawkins, we sat for many hours while ministering at his church in Albuquerque, talking about these things, especially his own experience of the Eucharist. His deep insights into the subject have been profoundly encouraging, especially regarding the 'fourth cup' and recommending the book *Jesus and the Jewish Roots of the Eucharist* by Brant Pitre.

To the **Thursday morning group** here in Bandera, TX, made up of those we count as sons and daughters and our staff, and to those who Zoom with us on Sundays have also come to know Andrew, Marshall, and Clint. We've spent hours discussing various chapters in the book and our shared growth in understanding these matters. A few months ago, I shared that our Eucharist service no longer reflected what we had come to see of the Gospel. I suggested we each privately review the service and update it if necessary. The following Thursday, Andrew had rewritten the entire service, and our hearts immediately bore witness to it. There were tears of joy as the words resonated with our spirits, and we stopped to celebrate with the new service. We now use it every Sunday, to the joy of everyone. I asked Andrew to write a chapter at the end of this book, and we've included the service for all of you to use.

I have had close fellowship with **Gabe Smith** in Sherman, TX, for many years as I worked through the pages you will soon read. Thank you for your simple yet profound insights!

To the many **pastors across the U.S. and Canada** I spoke with in the 1970s and 80s, whose names I may have forgotten. Some of you may recall the late-night conversations about the Eucharist and, in a few cases, allowing me to share a Eucharist service with your church.

To the **priests and bishops, past and present, of the Charismatic Episcopal Church**, for our rich fellowship in the Holy Spirit and sharing your insights into the Eucharist. You remain a part of my life that will never be forgotten, especially **Bishop Ken Myers**.

To the **monks of the Greek Orthodox Monastery** in Pennsylvania, who opened my eyes to a deeper understanding of the Holy Trinity.

To the **young men** who traveled with me from the 70s to the 90s, you carried my cases and made airports and ticketing easier for me. But the best times were the dinners after the service, talking late into the night, which resulted in **Michael Welchert** having a successful ministry and now being part of our extended staff in Colorado.

I traveled the world during the same period, with the help of **Gene Lilly**, who had received a miraculous healing years before, and we traveled the world together. Our long conversations in airports and jungle huts—from Hong Kong to Africa, India to the Philippines, and Malaysia—always centered around the Eucharist, and I remember them with grateful joy. Gene became a Bishop in the Philippines until he went to be with the Lord. Thank you, Gene—you fully understood!

Every few months, my wife and I travel to Houston, where some of her family lives, and I make sure to have lunch with **Don Keathley**, usually at Taste of Texas. We talk through lunch and into the afternoon, when Cheryl usually joins us. It is a blessing beyond words to share the great truths of grace and the love of God, and to hear Don's insights into the Eucharist.

Thank you, all!

Contents

Prologue

Some years ago, I was interviewed on a Christian radio station, and the interviewer asked if I would describe the most important things I did in the work of my ministry. I could have answered that everything was subservient to one end: knowing Jesus, the Lord, the source and content of all life and ministry. But I knew what the interviewer was asking, so I replied, "I would not be who I am in this moment without the Holy Spirit as my lifelong Friend, the One who opened my inner eyes to see the truth, the One who is the power and ability to put into practice what He revealed to me. I also give great place to the Scriptures, to the point where I memorized the New Testament in my late teens and into my twenties, and then many portions of the Old Testament."

The interviewer nodded to that part of my answer, but then I said, "I also partake of the Eucharist every week and sometimes many times in the week." At this, she looked mildly shocked and said, "I was not aware that you were a Roman Catholic!" to which I replied, "I am not a Roman Catholic, but then, I am not a Protestant either! The word Protestant means 'one who protests,' and I do not define myself by what I am not, but by who I am in Christ."

The Eucharist does not belong to any one sector of Christianity; some may call it the Meal, Holy Communion, the Lord's Supper, or the Last Supper. Each name highlights a different aspect of this sacred Meal.

> I call it the *Meal of Wonder*, the *Meal of Mystery*. I also use the word *Eucharist*, which comes to us from the early days of the church and means *The Thanksgiving*—which indeed it is.

I have not written this book to provoke anger from theologians or religious church leaders, nor to call anyone to take sides in explaining what happens to the bread and wine at the celebration—taking sides usually leads to a theological brawl! Instead, I am sharing with you my own journey, one that began with asking questions as a teenager and continues to this day. That journey was marked by insights into passages of Scripture and a deeper understanding of specific words, shedding light on the path I was on at that time. With each new revelation, I often believed I had reached the end of my search, yet the Spirit continually beckoned me toward more than I had ever anticipated! Now, as I celebrate my 86th birthday, we celebrate the Eucharist every week as a body of believers—and many times, I celebrate it every day, either alone or with my wife.

I invite you to join me in a journey that meanders through decades of searching—a journey not directed by any person or denomination, but one where I listened to the Holy Spirit and the plain words of Scripture.

There are multitudes whom I trust will read this book, who are aptly described by Tolkien in *Lord of the Rings*, but this description can be applied to myself as I began the journey, which rapidly became an adventure, and still applies to many who will join this adventure, seeking holy treasure that has been buried from multitudes over the centuries.

> *"Much that once was is lost, for none lived who could remember it. Some things that should not have been forgotten were lost. History became legend and legend became myth."* (TOLKIEN IN *LORD OF THE RINGS*)

1. Crackers and Grape Juice

My eyes were first opened to the ascended Lord Jesus when I was entering my teenage years, around the age of twelve. I had not grown up attending church, nor had I knowingly seen a Bible. Although we had Bible readings and prayers every morning in British public schools, I still did not know the Book they were reading from, nor did I understand to whom they were speaking when heads were bowed and eyes were closed.

I was dragged into Sunday school by a concerned neighbor, where I heard the Gospel for the first time. I went into a private room with the Sunday school teacher, and we prayed together, and I asked Jesus into my life.

My testimony affected my mother, and we both set out to find a church. We ended up at the Elim Pentecostal Church, part of a group of churches that sprang from the revival that spread across the world in the early 20th century. They believed that every believer should know and experience the Spirit, just as Jesus had said. The Spirit was to be the Friend, Teacher, Guide, Mentor, and personal Coach to every believer. He is the One who awakens the heart of every person, revealing the living Jesus in their lives. The gifts of the Spirit, listed and demonstrated in the New Testament, were expected to be the experience of the local church.

In a short while, I experienced the Spirit in the most personal way and was now filled with enthusiasm, ready for all He was about to teach me. I was learning to know the Spirit in both my life at home and in school. It was the beginning of knowing Him as my true Friend, my Guide, and Teacher—and the rest of my life has been defined by Him.

The church met every Sunday morning for a service that focused entirely on Holy Communion. Strangers were not encouraged to attend unless they were believers; there was no invitations for unbelievers to accept Christ. The focus was solely on one thing: the Meal that Jesus had instituted the night He was betrayed.

> "For I received from the Lord that which I also delivered to you, that the Lord Jesus, on the night when He was betrayed, took bread; and, when He had given thanks, He broke it and said, 'This is My body, which is for you; do this in remembrance of Me.' In the same way, *He* also *took* the cup after supper, saying, "This cup is the new covenant in My blood; do this, as often

> as you drink *it*, in remembrance of Me." For as often as you eat this bread and drink the cup, you proclaim the Lord's death until He comes." 1 Corinthians 11:23-26

There were several hymns—all of them focused on the sufferings and death of Jesus, aiming to awaken our imagination fulfill what Jesus had said: *"Do this in remembrance of Me."* As we sang these solemn hymns, we struggled to imagine the blood-shed and sufferings of Jesus on the cross.

I did not understand the Sunday morning Meal of Communion. My head was filled with questions. First, it was called a meal—which puzzled me, as it consisted of a tiny glass of grape juice that nearly spun out of my hand, along with a small piece of cracker no bigger than my thumbnail. It seemed strange to call that a meal! But I let it be.

But a piece of bread and a sip of wine did not fit in my mind with the great truths of the Gospel, which we studied in Bible study services and groups that explored the great doctrines of the faith—those invisible, spiritual, and eternal matters. It almost seemed like an insult to study such deep spiritual matters that came to a finale in this sip of grape juice and tiny, bit of a cracker! I could not fathom where this broken cracker and sip of juice fit into the high and holy spiritual matters we were introduced to in the weekly Bible study and our study groups!

But then came questions that confronted the very root of what we were doing. Every week, before we ate and drank the Meal, the pastor read the words of Jesus: *"Do this in remembrance of Me."* I wanted to shout, "Stop! Time out!" These words demanded an answer to make sense of the service.

To me, it was as nonsensical as trying to remember a vacation we took in China before we were born! I was told that the sad hymns, meant to evoke an imagination of His sufferings, were the remembrance. I countered that *remembering* had little to do with imagination; none of us present had the slightest idea what crucifixion by Roman soldiers looked like two thousand years ago! How could we possibly imagine it?

Our imagination was continually directed to the sufferings and death of Jesus, yet He had said, "Do this in remembrance of Me." Why had we taken one episode of His life (of supreme importance, I grant you) and called it "Me"? Surely *Me* includes not just His birth, life, and death, but also His resurrection and ascension!

But that was nothing compared to the pastor holding up the cracker and grape juice and saying, "This is My body, this is My blood," followed by a brief statement assuring us that Jesus didn't really mean it literally; it was just a way to help us remember His death. I thought that was a very strange aid to imagining suffering and death!

But I countered in my mind: if He said it was His body and blood, then surely He meant it! If not, why didn't He do what the pastor did every Sunday and tell us that He didn't really mean it, and that we were simply to take it as a strange aid in remembering His sufferings and death?

The pastor was, in fact, inserting the brutal history of England during the great persecutions between Protestants and Catholics in the 16th and 17th centuries over this very issue. He seemed more concerned that we not believe Jesus actually meant what He said.

I put it on the back burner, as no one could answer me; my questions only seemed to anger them. So I settled in every Sunday morning, taking the tiny glass of grape juice and piece of broken cracker, consuming it in a few seconds—and calling it a feast!

I moved from my hometown, but wherever I attended Sunday morning church, the same words were spoken, and the same questions rose within me—only to be dismissed as having no answer that would satisfy me.

Eventually, I became a pastor of a small church on the east coast of England and had to conduct a Sunday morning service according to the denominational service book. I left out the rabid Protestant explanation of His body and blood being a mistaken statement.

Still, the question remained: what did Jesus mean when He said this piece of bread and cup of wine were His body and blood? Was this sip of grape juice and broken cracker really His body and blood? Some laughed at my question as being ridiculous; others cautioned me not to delve into such questions. But to me, it still tasted like crackers and grape juice!

In my twenties, I moved to the U.S., and the first thing that struck me was Sunday morning: no communion services! In fact, the entire Sunday service was focused on unbelievers, with a program tailored to that end. The other services during the week were brief, offering little for believers—and certainly no communion.

One Sunday, while preaching my way across the Western States, I was surprised by the announcement that it was communion Sunday! The same tiny glasses appeared, though this time they were plastic, but the grape juice and crackers were the same. The pastor altered the words of Jesus; instead of saying, "This is My body and blood," he said, "This represents My body and blood." There is a massive difference between *is* and *represents*. Jesus didn't say that the bread and wine were merely an aid to our memory by somehow representing His suffering body and shed blood!

The deacons distributed the plastic cups and crackers along each row, followed by helpers with trash bags to collect the empty cups after the benediction was announced. I barely had time to reflect on any of my questions—it was over so quickly. Before I knew it, we were standing outside in the sunlight, without even a hymn to conclude the service.

At another service of Holy Communion, the pastor began urgently telling us to examine ourselves, lest we eat and drink with sin in our lives and end up becoming deathly ill or dropping dead, falling directly into hell! No wonder most of the crackers and juice were left untouched!

Since arriving in the States and getting used to either no communion service or one or two scattered throughout the year, I was shocked to find that I missed the weekly service as we had celebrated in England!

It wasn't the same kind of missing as when I longed for parts of English life that were no longer available in the U.S.—like my morning cup of tea or walking half a mile to get the newspaper. I ached for those things every time a passing car threw a gigantic roll of newspaper into our driveway! But this missing was different. There was a deep sense of emptiness, as though a vital part of my life was missing. I felt a strange hunger for the service I had never truly appreciated or understood.

The five-minute communion service, tagged onto the main service, didn't meet my now-felt need. Instead, it unexpectedly pointed out that something—or rather, Someone—had been quietly at work during those Sunday mornings in England, beyond my intellectual understanding. The church I attended at the time would be called Charismatic. We were used to the Spirit overwhelming people and revealing Jesus in a life-changing way, but this experience of the Spirit wasn't overwhelming—it was invisible, silent, and, I would have to say, *mysterious*. The Holy Spirit fed us in our deepest spirit through that weekly strange Meal called Holy Communion.

> My questions remained unanswered, but now I added another: *"What had been taking place that I now had to admit had fed my spirit, despite my brain's attempts to turn it into a debate, if not an argument?"*

It also occurred to me that it was worth considering that, however minimal, there was still a service of bread and wine at all. After Jesus instituted the Meal 2,000 years ago, we were still conducting a service—something that, though only remotely like the original, persisted. If it were meaningless, surely it would have disappeared from church practice long ago.

I set out to discover the meaning and place of Holy Communion—the Eucharist.

2. The Mystery of the Gospel

"Let a man regard us in this manner, as servants of Christ and stewards (guardians) of the *mysteries of God."* 1 Corinthians 4:1

"By common confession, great is the *mystery of godliness:* He who was revealed in the flesh, was vindicated in the Spirit, seen by angels, proclaimed among the nations, believed on in the world, taken up in glory." 1 Timothy 3:16

Driving along an interstate the other day, I saw a large billboard depicting a young man with his head in his hands, the picture of despair. Beside the image was a line: "At the end of your rope? Try Jesus!" I remembered that, some years ago, it was common to take an advertising jingle and substitute Jesus for the product, calling people to *try Him*, as if He were merely one among many possible solutions! The Gospel becomes a religious Madison Avenue, asking you to at least give Jesus a try and see if it works! But Jesus cannot be sold like a can of Coke! We are not seeking votes to establish that He is the Lord and Savior!

It is here that we confront the word *mystery* and various words terms: *made known, manifested, revealed, proclaimed,* and *understand.* We must forget the common English usage of *mystery* which refers to something hidden that challenges even the sharpest minds to unravel and discover what has been concealed from us. It usually means that the average person cannot fathom the mystery, and everyone waits for a mental wizard who can figure it out.

The Gospel—the faith that comes to us in and through Jesus Christ and handed down to us through the apostles—is often called the Mystery. This does not mean the Gospel is a detective story waiting for our or someone's intellect to unravel it.

In Scripture, *mystery* does not refer to something unknowable challenging our intellect to fathom its secret. It means a truth that has been hidden or covered, one that cannot be uncovered or explained by human reason or logic. The word in the New Testament means something that was hidden *but is now revealed through Jesus Christ.* The Holy Spirit is the Guide and Teacher who opens our inner eyes to see Jesus plainly, the key and meaning to all mysteries.

The mysteries include the Incarnation, the life of Jesus Christ, His death and resurrection, and His dwelling within us through the Holy Spirit. Our unassisted intellect cannot begin to understand any of those events' vital words of the Gospel.

The Spirit is the One who uncovers and reveals the Gospel. We cannot hope to discover the Gospel apart from the Holy Spirit. We do not come to the Gospel with intellect primed to understand the Triune God who loves us! The Spirit is the One who opens our inner eyes of the heart and applies the revelation in our personal lives, in our neighbor's eyes as we share Jesus, or the evangelist preaching the Gospel.

Our theological degrees are useless here! Jesus gave His longest message (John 14-16) telling us of the need to depend on the Spirit, our Teacher and Guide into all truth.

> "At that time, Jesus said, "I praise You, Father, Lord of heaven and earth, that You have hidden these things from the wise and intelligent and have revealed them to infants. Yes, Father, for this way was well-pleasing in Your sight. All things have been handed over to Me by My Father; and no one knows the Son except the Father, *nor does anyone know the Father except the Son, and anyone to whom the Son wills to reveal Him."*
> Matthew 11:25-27

Jesus makes much of this fellowship with the Father. understanding comes not by intellectual ability but by the revelation given by the Spirit. He then makes the statement that no one knows the Son (Himself) except the Father, and *nor does anyone know the Father except the Son, and anyone to whom the Son wills to reveal Him.*

That means that when we know who Jesus the Son truly is, it is because we have been given divine revelation. Likewise, when we know the Father, it is because Jesus the Son has shared His unique knowledge with us. It is not the one trusting in their own intellect who knows, but those who trust in the Trinity to show us what otherwise would be hidden from us.

Jesus also gave us elements of creation to use them in applying the finished work of Jesus to our lives as believers. These creature elements include water, oil, bread, and wine, along with the laying on of our hands to heal the sick and impart special grace —created elements set apart to be the means by which the Holy Spirit works mysteriously, wonderfully, invisibly, and silently in our whole being. These, too, are part of the mysteries opening pathways of grace, leading us directly to Jesus Christ to feed and nourish our inner person.

These mysteries include the Eucharist. *The Eucharist* is the Greek word that comes to us from the earliest ages of the church. The word means *the Great Thanksgiving*, known also as *the Holy Communion* and *the Lord's Supper*. The Eucharist plays a vital part in our living this life in Christ.

These mysteries could be called physical faith because we use the created elements—water, oil, bread, and wine—to engage all our physical senses as we exercise our trust in Him and His finished work. In them, we meet the Person of the ascended Christ. Let me underscore that we meet with Him—not encase Him in doctrine, not separate His words to become dead morality, not think about, not try to imitate, but *meet* Him, know Him, and awaken to our union with Him.

This, unashamedly, is the wonder of all wonders! The word *wonder* in Scripture means impossible for the human mind to think, let alone do, but speaks of the work of God, a miracle or a marvel, a marvelous thing.

Bandera Creek runs through our ranch here in Texas, and I have spent many hours meditating on its banks. One day, I was watching a frog sunning itself on a rock. As I watched, without warning, it collapsed into a flat skin on the rock! It was then that I became aware of a water bug that had inserted its teeth into the back of the frog and literally sucked its insides out! That water bug is a picture of religion! Religion sucks the life, the wonder, the breathtaking marvel out of the Gospel, leaving us with a dead husk—just words and pious attempts to be like Jesus but without life—dead!

This must not be thought of as God deliberately hiding the saving knowledge of the Gospel from anyone! What it tells us is that this precious knowledge is not found in our unassisted intellect working to know but is revealed to us only by the Spirit in Jesus Christ. In the Matthew passage quoted above, Jesus goes on to tell us whom He reveals the Father to.

> "Come to Me, all who are weary and
> heavy-laden, and I will give you rest.
> Take My yoke upon you and learn
> from Me, for I am gentle and humble
> in heart, and you will find rest for your
> souls. For My yoke is easy, and My
> burden is light." Matthew 11:28-30

A well-known text, but rarely connected to those to whom Jesus reveals divine truth.

In the following chapters, we are pursuing the meaning and place of the Eucharist, and I want to establish from the beginning that the Holy Spirit must be our Guide, leading us into all truth and opening our eyes to the mystery. We do not bring our best reasoning or logic to understand the Meal that Jesus instituted, but rely on the Spirit to give us the gift of insight and divine light and to open the eyes of our understanding to begin to see the vastness of His love and limitless accomplishment of salvation in Christ.

On the evening of the resurrection, two disciples, dragging their feet in despair, unable to make sense of the crucifixion of the One they believed to be the Messiah, were going back to their home in Emmaus to attempt to pick up the pieces and move forward. Jesus, freshly risen from the dead, came alongside them in the appearance of a traveler. He initiated a conversation in which He unveiled the Old Testament Scriptures, showing that Messiah had to die at the hands of wicked men and rise again from the dead. They later reported that their hearts had burned within them as He spoke. As they approached their house, they constrained Him to come in and to continue sharing with them.

At dinner, He assumed the position of the host, reached for the bread, gave thanks, broke it, and in that moment, they recognized Him. He immediately was gone from their sight. they were overwhelmed with wonder and joy and rushed back to Jerusalem to tell the other disciples. They summed up their report by saying, "He was *made known to us* in the breaking of bread!" They were not convinced of the resurrection by an intellectual argument; it was made known when the cover was lifted, and they realized it was the living Jesus they were fellowshipping with! Their inner eyes were opened to see Him alive in their house at supper, in the breaking of bread, just as He had broken it in the rooftop room in Jerusalem the previous Thursday night. Although His teaching was vital to them, causing their hearts to burn, it was in the breaking of bread, the Meal He instituted in the upper room, that the mystery was uncovered, and they knew Him clearly, the risen Messiah.

That same night, He appeared to the gathered disciples and 'opened their minds' so that they might have a clear revelation of the new world the Gospel brought.

To awaken to the Gospel is to embrace the supernatural—from incarnation through His resurrection and ascension, there is nothing that can be merely heard and believed as a fact of history at an intellectual level. The same applies to the Eucharist. In the following pages, we will, unapologetically, be confronted by the supernatural, the work of the Spirit in our everyday lives. The Gospel is not merely the report of historic events concerning

Jesus of Nazareth, but the announcement that He is alive, with us, in us, and the unchanged and unchanging Savior of all men and women.

The New Testament portrays life and everything we do, whatever that may be, not as an impersonal formula or a ten-step program, but as the Person of Christ Himself—all in all. He is at the center of life—and the meaning of life. Paul said, "For me to live is Christ," and "Christ who is my life." This is how the first believers understood their life.

3. Chaos in Capernaum

It was sometime in the spring, about a year before Jesus went to the cross and rose from the dead. The season of Passover had arrived—a time for eating the sacred meal, celebrating with joy the nation's deliverance from slavery in Egypt, and retelling the story of God's mighty act of salvation through the symbols of bread and wine.

These were exciting days, filled with crowds eagerly gathering to hear Jesus' words and the multitudes of sick being healed of every disease. At this time, Jesus enjoyed immense popularity, especially in the North around Lake Galilee. It was there, in the hills and in the town of Capernaum, that Jesus spoke words that would spark a crisis in His ministry—words that would cause the people to turn against Him, dismissing Him as a madman. Words that could have brought His ministry to a halt!

The risk He took in speaking as He did alerts us to the fact that this must be among the most important things that Jesus had to share. These words could, and in fact did, do damage to His entire mission! One might wonder whether He could have kept these words to Himself or reserved them for His closest disciples. What necessity compelled Him to speak to the vast crowds, knowing He would lose the goodwill of these simple peasants and common people?

The only conclusion is that they were, and are, words of the highest importance—words that must be said for His message to be fully grasped. If the subject was a matter of religious curiosity, merely footnotes to His main message, then He would surely have left them unspoken.

It is significant that He set them up for this conversation with the feeding of the multitude the previous evening. He planned to give this message to the peasants of Galilee; He never spoke of it to the proud religious intellectuals of Jerusalem and the Temple. These words, which seemed to jeopardize His entire mission, were spoken to His friends—the peasant folk of Galilee—who had joyfully responded to His message and received healing miracles at His hands.

Galilee was the place He called home. Jesus weighed the importance of the message and determined that His best friends and constant audience could go no further in their relationship with Him without hearing and accepting these words as foundational to His mission, revealing who He was and what He had come to do.

Predictably, this short message in the synagogue in Capernaum was the end of His popularity; the people of the Galilee, sadly, shook their heads, turned their backs on Him, and walked away.

The previous day, He had spoken to a vast crowd in the hills on the other side of the lake. He had taught them, healed their sick folk, and then had very deliberately set them up for the miraculous picnic, feeding five thousand men along with their wives and children, with five loaves (probably tortillas!) and two fish.

When it dawned on the people that they had been fed with five lunch rolls and two little fish in a boy's lunch pail, they were caught up in a mass frenzy to make Him king of Israel. A leader who had miraculous powers would surely be the one to lead them against their Roman oppressors and bring about the long-awaited Kingdom of God. They sought to crown Him king there on the side of the mountain. He would not even discuss the possibility, but escaped from them, fleeing into the hills, and spent the rest of the evening and most of the night in prayer with His Father.

The people must learn that His kingdom is not after the order of this world; He had not come to set up a kingdom remotely like Rome or any other world power. Neither He, nor any He appointed, would look or be treated as an earthly monarch or president.

It was obvious that, no matter how long they had been with Him and loved what He said and did, they had not a clue of what He had come to do or who He was. He was not to be confused with the Roman Caesar—He had no grand palace, no crown of this world on His head, no cape adorned with this world's bling! He had not come to conquer with sword and bloodshed, nor did He desire groveling slaves crawling to Him, wailing that they were worthless and begging for mercy. His purpose in being here was beyond their wildest dreams. He came to deliver them from the bondage of sin and darkness and to unite their lives with His!

In the middle of the night, He came down from the mountain and walked on the stormy waves of the Lake to the little fishing boat where His disciples battled the winds. They were terrified and fell to the deck, worshiping Him as the Son of God.

The next morning, the crowd from the night before—who had wanted Him to be *their version* of Messiah King—searched for Him around the hills where the miracle of the loaves and fishes took place, and they had last seen Him. When they finally found Him in Capernaum, on the other side of the lake, they were confused as to how He got there without a boat!

They followed Him into the synagogue in a confused state of mind. Jesus gently accused them of picking up where they left off the previous evening, still wanting Him to produce more signs and lead them to a supernatural military victory over the Roman army of occupation—as a leader like Moses. The conversation turned to Moses, who had given manna, the mystery bread from heaven, that fed the people throughout their journey through the wilderness. Moses gave them the manna as a sign of God being with him, and now they looked to Jesus for such a sign! If He had come down from heaven as He claimed, then let Him give them a sign like the one Moses gave!

Jesus assured them they needed a Bread infinitely greater than the manna, the Bread that Moses gave them. Jesus was the Bread of Life.

> "For the bread of God is that which comes down out of heaven and gives life to the world." Then they said to Him, "Lord, always give us this bread." Jesus said to them, "I am the bread of life; he who comes to Me will not hunger, and he who believes in Me will never thirst. But I said to you that you have seen Me, and yet do not believe. All that the Father gives Me will come to Me, and the one who comes to Me I will certainly not cast out. For I have come down from heaven, not to do My own will, but the will of Him who sent Me. This is the will of Him who sent Me, that of all that He has given Me I lose nothing, but raise it up on the last day. For this is the will of My Father, that everyone who beholds the Son and believes in Him will have eternal life, and I Myself will raise him up on the last day." John 6:33-40

Jesus pointed out that those ancestors, even though they had eaten the miraculous manna, still died in the wilderness.

> "Truly, truly, I say to you, it is not Moses who has given you the bread out of heaven, but it is My Father who gives

> you the true bread out of heaven. For the bread of God is that which comes down out of heaven and gives life to the world." Then they said to Him, "Lord, always give us this bread." John 6:32-34

The people quickly understood that if He was the Bread of Life that the manna had merely pointed to, and who would take away all hunger, who was the Source of true Life, then one must *eat of Him* as their forefathers ate manna.

They readily ate of the miraculous meal He provided the night before, indifferent to how it happened. But when He declared that He would give them His flesh to eat and His blood to drink, they dismissed Him as delusional—perhaps even a magician—leading them into unspeakable law-breaking and paganism. Unable to accept Him as more than just a man, they rose in anger.

At that point Jesus could have said that they have misunderstood His words, but He doesn't, because they have understood Him perfectly!

> "Then the Jews began to argue with one another, saying, 'How can this man give us His flesh to eat?'" John 6:52

Instead of steering them away from the idea of eating Him, He instead emphasized His words, repeating them so clearly no one could misunderstand!

> “Jesus said to them, "Truly, truly, I say to you, unless you eat the flesh of the Son of Man, and drink His blood, you have no life in yourselves. He who eats My flesh and drinks My blood has eternal life, and I will raise him up on the last day. For My flesh is true food, and My blood is true drink. He who eats My flesh and drinks My blood abides in Me, and I in him. As the living Father sent Me, and I live, because of the Father, so he who eats Me, he also will live because of Me. This is the bread which came down out of heaven; not as the fathers ate and died; he who eats this bread will live forever.” John 6:53-58

His words were not ambiguous. Unless a person ate and drank of His flesh and blood, they had no life in themselves; they were the walking dead!

Chaos erupted in the synagogue. What was this man saying? Was He promoting cannibalism? Loud murmurs rippled through the crowd. *Could Jesus really be telling them to eat Him?*

They stood in small groups, trying to make sense of His words. *Is Jesus out of His mind?* The audience was shocked, scandalized, angry, and disgusted. Many were pushing through the crowd, their rage evident in their expressions and loud statements of disgust as they stomped toward the door.

These simple peasants of Galilee were in total confusion; their heads were spinning, and their thoughts were incoherent. *Doesn't He know the Law forbids the drinking of blood? Are you telling us to break the Law and turn us into pagan cannibals?*

The crowd was standing and shouting, others were making straight for the door, while yet others were holding their children tightly, covering their ears, and hurrying them out of the building.

> *Let me emphasize again—Jesus could have stopped the exodus at any moment. He could have quieted the people, clarified His meaning, and assured them that His words weren't meant literally. But He did not!*

His support was draining out through the door, like the waters of the Jordan pouring into the Dead Sea! These were His peasant folk who thronged Him in marketplaces, beaches, and hillsides here in the North, now sadly exiting. Their beloved Jesus, the One who had healed them and spoken words of hope, had gone mad! They had thought Him to be sent from God, maybe Messiah, but now they turned toward home with a terrible sense of loss.

As the door slammed shut for the last time, Jesus stood at the front of the building with His few disciples, who, like everyone else, were shocked, confused, and embarrassed that it was their teacher who had said these things. He turned to them with no explanation.

Jesus pointed out that the real problem was not primarily what He said but that He spoke of Himself as coming down from heaven, having a heavenly origin, and giving Himself to be the Bread of Life. They saw Him as their neighbor; they knew His mother, Mary, and Joseph, whose only claim to fame was that he was the carpenter with the storefront down the street.

The miracles He performed in their streets and hillsides were somehow different; they did not know how He did them, but they were happy to receive them. But this was different! To offer Himself as life-giving food, infinitely more than Moses could give —that was moving toward blasphemy and certainly breaking the Law regarding the drinking of blood and moving them all to cannibalism!

They did not believe Him to be who He was and, therefore, rose in rage at what He claimed to do. Those who were left were from a number who would call themselves disciples, although not as close as the circle of the twelve. He knew they did not believe, although they struggled toward faith that could handle these words.

4. The Doorway to Life

"Truly, truly, I say to you, unless you eat the flesh of the Son of Man and drink His blood, you have no life in yourselves. He who eats My flesh and drinks My blood has eternal life, and I will raise him up on the last day." John 6:53-54

What did Jesus mean? He meant exactly what He said! This was the one conversation He could have softened to avoid confusion and offense, but He chose not to. When given the chance to clarify or retract, He underscored it instead!

When He spoke of His flesh and blood, He was speaking of His Incarnation. He who is the uncreated God from God, of one being with the Father, willed as one with the Father and the Spirit to come where we are, to be born of the Virgin Mary, assume our humanity, our flesh and blood bodies, born in a rush of blood and water as every human being. The cry of this Baby echoed through the streets of Bethlehem and across the fields, where the shepherds smiled and dismissed it as the announcement of another member of the race taking his first gulp of oxygen! No one realized that the cry was the cry of God Incarnate, becoming our flesh, the beginning of the fulfillment of all the ancient promises and prophecies of God's salvation.

Incarnation meant God, in His infinite love, refused to let us return to the nothingness from which He called us. He refused to be God without humanity enjoying the relationship He created us for. Incarnation means that He had come to seek us, into our broken flesh, into our darkness, the web of lies regarding the character of God and our human identity. He came seeking us, behind all our barriers erected against Him, to fulfill the plan the Trinity had purposed to bring mankind home to the Father. He became one of us; He became the totality of mankind, and He lived and worked as a Galilean peasant, none of His neighbors dreaming who He really was. He is God, being God *as human.* This is not a man trying to be like God but God being Himself while simultaneously being human.

He is not calling us to eat of God, the invisible Spirit, untouched by the troubles and temptations we face as humans, but to eat of His flesh and blood, which He assumed in His incarnation. He lived as man-who-is-God in the limitations, pains, and joys—the darkness of the lie—facing Him at every turn, which He overcame by keeping His eyes on His Father and ears open to His truth. He now says, in vivid language, that we can eat Him—participate in His divine human life!

So, which *flesh and blood are we to eat?* The flesh and blood of Galilee and Jerusalem? Jesus of Bethlehem, of Nazareth, of Capernaum, where He healed the sick and cast out demons in the Gospel accounts of His life?

No, that would indeed be cannibalism—eating another human! It would also be illogical because that body was limited; if the crowd in Capernaum had eaten Him, He would have been quickly consumed and gone! If it was the body that was tortured by wicked men and taken to the cross and lowered to the tomb, we would be eating a mutilated dead corpse, recently taken down from the cross of humiliation and shame, bearing the sin of the world!

Jesus did not institute this Meal of eating Himself until the last minutes before He was arrested and taken to death. His body was not yet broken for us, His blood not yet shed. He spoke prophetic words that would be fulfilled that night and into the next day. His death was not the end and can never be thought of as the end!

His death signaled that His resurrection and ascension would soon be taking place next. The Person of Jesus, Living One, the triumphant life that came out of the tomb, that had destroyed death, put away sin, and welcomed us into the Father's House—this is the life that can never die, that has brought about the death of death!

His resurrected, ascended body that was no longer limited by time and space, but immediately present to every human throughout the world–*that body and blood He gives to us to eat,* and in so doing, we become one with the triumph of His cross that His resurrection won! We are to eat of His life that was given but who rose from the dead with everything for our salvation finished forever. This life of resurrection has opened the door for humans to come to and know the Father, eternal life.

LIFE THAT CANNOT DIE MUST FIRST DEFEAT DEATH.

Now we understand more clearly that to eat of Him was to have eternal life. He equates eating His flesh and drinking His blood to receiving and possessing eternal life.

We must understand the meaning of the word *eternal or everlasting.* The word *eternal* in Greek is *aeon.* Translating that word as *eternal* or *everlasting* has portrayed the life Jesus gives as something limited to after death, merely an extension of human life—a mere living forever in a dream place called heaven! It has turned 21st-century Christianity into an obsession with death and the afterlife! *But this is not what the word means.* A better translation would be that *we partake of the life of the ages, the life of God; we participate in the relationship of Father and Son, given to us through Jesus Messiah.*

> *"This is eternal life, that they may know You, the only true God, and Jesus Christ whom You have sent."* John 17:3

That they may know You. The word 'know' is not to be confused with merely knowing **about** someone or a subject—this word describes the *personal experience* of someone—two lives in seamless union, the relationship between two persons in covenant. It is used throughout Scripture to describe the marriage union.

A union so real that it is aptly described as eating Him—participating in His life without losing ourselves in Him. We eat of Him, yet He, who is revealed as God in our glorified human body, is neither consumed nor diminished! No other words could so completely describe the wonder of the salvation He spoke of.

He describes this as a *constant being at home, dwelling, abiding in Him.* This is not a one-time event but a continual realization, participating in His life hour by hour in the home, school, work, in this world.

This is the mission His Father sent Him to accomplish, and He tied it together with eating His body and drinking His blood. Unlike eating the manna, it resulted in the most intimate relationship with God—Father, Son, and Spirit. A relationship that sent the mind spinning and the imagination reaching, trying to grasp the wildest of dreams! Humans eat the flesh of the glorified, incarnate God, and thus most literally participate in the life of God in Christ.

The Meal does not celebrate His dying but His resurrection after having conquered death! We do not come as groveling sinners to partake but as forgiven, cleansed, redeemed, and reconciled children through His body given and His blood shed.

> *"And although you were formerly alienated and hostile in mind, engaged in evil deeds, yet He*

> *has now reconciled you in His fleshly body through death, in order to present you before Him holy and blameless and beyond reproach.*" Colossians 1:21-22

Or as the Mirror Study Bible translates these same verses:

> "Your indifferent mindset alienated you from God, into a lifestyle of annoyances, hardships, and labors. Yet He has now fully reconciled and restored you to your original design. He accomplished this in dying our deaths in a human body; He fully represented us in order to fully present us again in blameless innocence, face-to-face with God; with no sense of guilt, suspicion, regret, or accusation; all charges against us are officially canceled." Colossians 1:21-22 (Mirror Bible)

I say again, the trouble in the synagogue in Capernaum centered on seeing and hearing Him as a man, a neighbor, the carpenter down the street, the son of Mary and Joseph—how could He say such things? If one knows this One is none other than God in our flesh, then one does not spew anger at Him but stands in awe of this Person who is fully Man and fully God, who therefore can feed us with His flesh and blood.

He goes as far as to say that the relationship He had with His Father is parallel to the one He was describing as eating His flesh. He lived minute by minute from the Father's life, and those who eat His flesh now live minute by minute from that same life of God, available in the glorified, incarnate flesh of Jesus the Christ.

This life that He came to give was not an external gift, a package that was separate from Him and merely given by Him! *The Gift was the Giver*—partaking of the life of Jesus, as He would say later as He went to the giving of His flesh and shedding of His blood, *"I in you and you in Me."*

This was shocking, even nauseating, to the people, and to many today. But the truth is we all entered the world in this fashion. From conception for nine months, we literally ate of our mother's life! Everything she ate, we ate through her; every thought she had, every drink she consumed, every drug she took, and all that she listened to in conversation or the media became ours through her blood. After birth, we continued to eat of her through her breasts. We ate of her, and our life depended on that nourishment!

In my search for the meaning of the Eucharist, these verses arrested me. Multi thousands of believers today have the same problem that the crowd had as they exited the synagogue. Instead of trusting Jesus, like the few remaining disciples did, many today respond with a simple answer that justifies walking away—*Jesus did not mean what He said! He meant something much more sensible and palatable! Change His words and forget He ever ruined His reputation by talking of such things!*

When, as a teenager, I began to ask questions about John 6, the Bible scholars smiled knowingly and took me to John 6:60-64:

> “Therefore many of His disciples, when they heard this said, "This is a difficult statement; who can listen to it?" But Jesus, conscious that His disciples grumbled at this, said to them, "Does this cause you to stumble? What then if you see the Son of Man ascending to where He was before? It is the Spirit who gives life; the flesh profits nothing; the words that I have spoken to you are spirit and are life. But there are some of you who do not believe." For Jesus knew from the beginning who they were who did not believe, and who it was that would betray Him.” John 6:60-64

I was seriously told that Jesus was now telling the larger group of His disciples that everything He had said about eating His flesh in the previous verses was canceled by these words! Did it not plainly say, 'the flesh profits nothing'? Therefore, they claimed, He was only speaking of repenting and believing in Him in this extreme way. That made no sense! This is not how Jesus speaks in any of His discourses—He doesn’t stir up such an emotional response only to say, 'I didn’t mean it, cancel it all!'

I had to hear what He was saying before I could go any further. The first words that arrest us are how He describes Himself, not on that day, but on a day in the future, after He had risen from the dead. He was saying, “You are offended by what I have said here but what will you do when you see the Son of Man ascending to where He was before?" That sentence is dense with reference to who He is and the day it will be revealed who He is.

His favorite title that He took to Himself was 'Son of Man,' which is taken from the prophet Daniel, chapter 7, and is a title that most Jews of that time understood to be the Messiah. In the prophecy, He is described as a divine person, yet also as a man coming *from* the earth *to* the heavens, where He receives the kingdom or rule of God in the Spirit, which extends to every family on earth—indeed, to all of humanity.

> "I kept looking in the night visions, and behold, with the clouds of heaven One like a Son of Man was coming, and He came up to the Ancient of Days and was presented before Him. And to Him was given dominion, glory, and a kingdom, that all the peoples, nations, and *men of every* language might serve Him. His dominion is an everlasting dominion which will not pass away; And His kingdom is one which will not be destroyed"... 'Then the sovereignty, the dominion, and the greatness of *all* the kingdoms under the whole heaven will be given to the people of the saints of the Highest One; His kingdom *will be* an everlasting kingdom, and all the dominions will serve and obey Him."
> Daniel 7:13-14, 27

Jesus is revealing Himself to these confused disciples as the Man-who-is-God who, although to be held by the great monster Rome, shall overcome it and overcome death, and rise from its clutches, and come to the Father and receive the kingdom of God to rule over all people. That kingdom is described in Romans 14 as being in the Spirit.

> "...for the kingdom of God is not eating and drinking, but righteousness and peace and joy in the Holy Spirit."
> Romans 14:17

He references 'The Son of Man'—a favorite expression Jesus used to describe Himself. More importantly, it is taken from the prophet Daniel in chapter 7. This was a clear description of the Messiah, who would ascend from the terrible beast (commonly identified as the Roman Empire) to God the Father, referred to by the prophet as 'The Ancient of Days.' The Messiah would take His place co-equal with the Father and become Lord over the entire world, being revealed as God. When the High Priest was desperately trying to find damning evidence to condemn Jesus to death, he asked Him, "Are you the Messiah?" to which Jesus replied that *He, the Son of Man would ascend, come to the Father* (from Matthew 26:63-64). It was those words, quoting Daniel 7, that gave the High Priest what He wanted, and He condemned Jesus to death for blasphemy.

Returning to our text in John 6 (verse 62), Jesus plainly speaks of the Son of Man ascending to where He was before. In the Incarnation, He had taken on our human flesh without breaking His eternal relationship with the Father. He became flesh so that He might carry us through death to join Him in resurrection life, and, having done so, He would return from whence He came. It was in His glorified, resurrected body that He sent the Holy Spirit to bring the goal of salvation to everyone. He said more than once that His body contained within it the Life that had conquered death and taken away the authority of death.

> It is obvious that to be the Source of Life that cannot die—eternal life—One must first have defeated death.

Jesus was not offering His body and blood that stood before them in the synagogue, nor the body that had healed their sick over the last few months—He had not yet died and resurrected, conquering death! That would indeed have been cannibalism, eating a fellow human being. Nor was He referring to His body, beaten, torn, and fresh from the cross, as the feast He spoke of. He had only walked the path to death, laden with the sin of the world—He was not giving that back *to us*, but rather carrying it away *from us* into death! Again, that would have been cannibalism, eating His lifeless corpse.

> *If He had referred to His body and blood as it was then, or as it would be in His death, it would be limited to that one corpse, enough for only a few people to eat.*

The only body and blood that were now radiant with a kind of life never seen on earth before was the body that came out of the tomb—alive, having trampled death underfoot, and declaring that He would never die again. Death was dead! A heavenly body, no longer limited by time or space, that can be present to the entire world simultaneously—it is *that* ascended body He gives us to eat and drink. The Spirit, given in the ascension, makes this the food of eternal Life.

> "When I (John) saw Him, I fell at His feet like a dead man. And He placed His right hand on me, saying, "Do not be afraid; I am the first and the last, and the living One; and I was dead, and behold, I am alive forevermore, and I have the keys of death and of Hades." Revelation 1:17-18

It was at this time the Spirit was given:

> "This Jesus God raised up again, to which we are all witnesses. Therefore, having been exalted to the right hand of God, and having received from the Father the promise of the Holy Spirit, He has poured forth this which you both see and hear." Acts 2:32-33

Throughout Scripture, the flesh is portrayed as the existence in which life is centered in the body—its brain, intellect, pleasures, and the satisfaction of nerves, glands, and muscles—all leading inevitably to death. But suppose there is a life that is infinitely beyond brain cells, beyond any satisfaction found in the body, but coming directly from a relationship with God the Father, through Jesus Christ, in the Holy Spirit–a life, joy, and peace *that could not be taken from us at death? Death is no longer the obscene end of human existence; what we see as an end now is the glorious continuation of the life that is in Jesus!*

We must not confuse what Jesus said in verse 63 of John 6 with the earlier verses. In verse 63, Jesus speaks of *the* flesh, the existence we have seen that takes place solely within the boundaries of the flesh, the human body that profits nothing. This is the first time Jesus has spoken of this in the chapter. The other references (the entire discourse) are to '*My* flesh' *and are linked to the Life that cannot die.* The Spirit is the life that lives in, and lives from, Jesus Christ risen from the dead, a reality made possible at His resurrection and ascension.

Put together, Jesus is saying that the people cannot believe He is more than a peasant from Galilee and, therefore, cannot give us His flesh to eat. But when He rises from the dead, ascends to the Father, and is revealed as the One who came from God and returned to God as Lord of all—on that day, they will see God in His glorified, resurrected body, giving Himself as heavenly food for His people to eat.

When we come to the Meal, we are coming to the resurrected, ascended glorious Body and Blood that He can share with all and not be consumed and be present to all simultaneously so that however many, wherever they are, they are present at the great Feast of union, the Marriage supper of the Lamb!

The resurrected body of Jesus is the body in which the purpose of God from the beginning is finished. We do not leave this feast to wait for our salvation—there is no delay based on what we do. After His exaltation to the Father, He announces that *He is the First and the Last, the Beginning and the End.*

> What does that body of glory look like, and how does it differ from the body He lived in and went into death in?

Paul discusses this at length in 1 Corinthians 15…

> "But someone will say, "…with what kind of body do they come?" … That which you sow does not come to life unless it dies; and that which you sow, you do not sow the body which is to be, but a bare grain, perhaps of wheat or of something else. But God gives it a body just as He wished, and to each of the seeds a body of its own. All flesh is not the same flesh, but there is one flesh of men … (Paul enumerates the various flesh bodies within creation).
> So also is the resurrection of the dead. It is sown a perishable body, it is raised an imperishable body; it is sown in dishonor, it is raised in glory; it is sown in weakness, it is raised in power; it is sown a natural body, it is raised a spiritual body." (1 Corinthians 15:35-44)

We are now in the undeniable presence of the ascended Jesus! In Him and from Him, we receive and celebrate the triumphant power of His resurrection body.

Paul likens the natural body that goes into the grave to a seed, and the seed has no likeness to the fruit or flower that will come. The body of Jesus in His life, the body that bore the weight of sin, and the body laid in the tomb—torn and bruised to the point of being unrecognizable as a man—that body was the seed. The body that rose from the dead and walked out of the tomb is nothing like the seed, the mangled body of His death. His resurrection body is supernatural—having overcome death, nothing is impossible for Him! The power in which He now lives and moves is described as 'the exceeding greatness of His power' that raised Him from the dead.

The Jesus we meet, risen from the dead, is glorious and beautiful in love, gently dealing with Mary in the garden of the Tomb, taking Peter aside to speak to him after his denying Him, speaking gently with Saul of Tarsus giving him hope of a glorious future together with Him. Sin has been taken away, and we are free from guilt, cleansed by His shed blood. He is alive—the living proof that death is defeated forever. The One who rose in resurrection carried sin, guilt, and death to the grave, and they are no more. His body is transformed; it is no longer the body of weakness that hung helpless on the cross or was laid in the tomb. He is the living receipt, the guarantee that all He has done is forever finished.

He is no longer a flesh-and-blood human but the resurrected, glorified human and can be wherever He wills, carrying within Him the fullness of His victory in resurrection.

This is not a fleeting moment but an eternal reality—now and forever, we are free from sin and the power of death. His body is the body of life, and we live because His resurrection life is now in us! His body has come through death, carrying us in Him, and now stands with us, face to face with the Father. To eat of Him is to realize our union with Him, and in Him, with the Father. This is the final Amen, the way it is—end of debate!

When we eat of His body, this glorious body, we are taking in the fullness of salvation. It is not a wake to remember a dead friend but a wild, whirling dance of victory and accomplishment by God for us. It is the Shepherd shouting, "Rejoice with Me, I have found My sheep!" We leave the feast made strong with the life of the ascended Christ, sharing in His rule in the earth.

His blood offered to them as a drink horrified His audience for good reason. Leviticus stated beyond all question that it could not be drunk because the life was in the blood – to drink would be to drink the soul of another human being. *But that is what this is all about.* Jesus was offering us His *resurrected blood*, called the blood of God, to drink—filled with the Spirit of Life that had conquered death and which was shed specifically for the life of the world.

> "So also it is written, "The first man, Adam, became a living soul." The last Adam (Jesus) became a life-giving spirit." 1 Corinthians 15:45

It was His custom to explain parables to the disciples after the crowd had left. But this time, He didn't explain; instead, He gave permission to the twelve and those close to Him, also described as disciples, to leave if they were scandalized by His teaching and unable to accept it.

> "As a result of this many of His disciples withdrew and were not walking with Him anymore. So, Jesus said to the twelve, "You do not want to go away also, do you?" Simon Peter answered Him, "Lord, to whom shall we go? You

> have words of eternal life. We have believed and have come to know that You are the Holy One of God." John 6:66-69

This unusual way of handling the situation reinforces two things: *first, that this teaching was of such vast importance that He was willing to let even His closest disciples leave if they could not accept it; second, it forever settled whether Jesus meant what He said in this and other Scriptures that speak of the same truth.*

Peter's words—"Lord, to whom shall we go? You have the words of life,"—emphasize that the storm surrounding these words is not calmed by a formula or by finally arriving at the right doctrine, but by a relationship—knowing, trusting, and living from (eating and drinking) Jesus, the very One who caused all the chaos!

5. Remember Me...

"Do this in remembrance of Me... "

Those words left me confused every time I heard them said at a communion service. *How can anything or anyone be remembered if we were not there?* Only in the sense that we remember an event of ancient history but there is no life in that exercise—it's merely the construction of a past event with the help of historians!

The word, as understood in the Western world, means going through boxes of memories like faded photos or papers needing sorting, all stored in our mind where we shuffle through, trying to find the appropriate page or image with which to reconstruct an event, something said, or someone's face-a vacation we took-with the help of our imagination. It is patchy, and two people will have two different memories of the same event.

That definition is where I was stuck. We were not present for the events of Jesus' life, death, or resurrection—*so how can we remember?*

The day I discovered that the word *remember* in the Bible languages is very different from how we understand it in the West was the day my life changed forever!

Instead of going back to excavate our memory, the word means to bring an event forward and redo it—replaying the event and, in so doing, releasing into the present moment the energy, promises, commands, joy, and strength of the original event. People who were not present at the original event could still be part of that remembrance.

It was a kind of time warp, where what *was* now becomes fresh and new, just as when it first took place.

In the daily life of those who lived in the Middle East, one might talk of remembering their wedding. The appropriate response would be "Let's do it!" The wedding would take place again, the vows renewed, and any friend could be present, who may or may not have been at the original wedding. People would be there remembering a wedding that they had not attended the first time!

Many of you are familiar with Zoom. We use it all the time in our ministry—100 or more join our Sunday morning service and are present at our meetings, though living in different countries, cities, and time zones.

When thinking about what happens in the celebration of the Eucharist, I began to compare it to Zoom. You are in your geographical place and time—*your now*. At the same instant, I am in my time and place—*my now*. As we both plug into Zoom, I am immediately in your geography and time without leaving mine—my now becomes your now and your now becomes mine. Though separated by thousands of miles and many hours, we are immediately present with one another, and we can communicate face to face!

This amazing connection is not limited to just one person, but a multitude simultaneously. On any given Sunday morning or during our Bible schools, I am present in the middle of the Pacific, in the U.K., across the Atlantic, in Venezuela, and in Africa—all at the same time. My now enters your now, sharing what is alive and true to me here.

Australia is an extreme example. They are a day ahead of Texas. I speak at 5 in the afternoon, and simultaneously they are listening and seeing me at 9 the following morning. It takes no time to travel across the Pacific to preach my message. I am speaking from their past, the previous night, but present to them in their now.

Here, at this moment, you are in many different time zones, but you are included in my time and my time becomes your time. From my time, I enter your time.

Our ability to Zoom is a marvel of modern technology, but it is only a faint illustration of how the Trinity is now. Just as Zoom collapses the barriers of time and space for our meetings, so does the Spirit collapse the distance between us and the ascended Jesus in the Eucharist.

> **Jesus is not a faded photo from 2,000 years ago; He is dynamically and invisibly present in all our times, and we in His time.** What He did is not ancient history but **present to us with Him.**

The early church welcomed newly baptized persons into the *eighth day*. They were saying that while time and space operates in seven days, we have now stepped beyond such limitations and are present to Father, Son, and Holy Spirit without reference to time or space. This means that He is present in millions of places at once, face to face with billions of people!

Jesus said it was to their supreme advantage that He went away so that the Spirit would come. When God became flesh, He was subject to time and space—if Jesus was in the Galilee and you, in Jerusalem, wanted a private moment with Him, you would have to travel some 70 miles north, hoping to find Him at the last place you heard He was, and take your place in line behind the multitude, who were also seek the same private time with Him! ***This is the genius of the Spirit, 'the greater works' He accomplishes. The Spirit*** takes us into the eighth day; He is present to us, and we are present to Him in all moments, and He is present to all who want such time with Him! And in the Spirit, we are present to the Father and the Son, our Lord Jesus Messiah!

Consider:

"I was crucified with Christ"

"We are seated in heavenly places," while sitting in office, and home

"That where I am you may be also"

"You may know…the exceeding greatness of His power…the same that raised Jesus from the dead"

"You who were dead in sin He made alive"

All these phrases refer to historical events that took place over 2,000 years ago on our historical timeline. However, understanding 'remember' means we are there, included in the event that has resulted in our life and behavior in the present!

The conversation in which this Meal was instituted just minutes before Jesus said, 'Do this in remembrance of Me,' went on to include His promise that the Holy Spirit would bring all things to their remembrance!

The word *remember* was used in everyday speech, but when we are dealing with our now dynamic communion with the risen, ascended Jesus, it takes on a new dimension. The Holy Spirit gives life into this definition, far beyond its ordinary usage.

The Spirit brings about the quiet wonder that we, in our present time and place, are present to the ascended Christ, just as He is present to us. All that He accomplished is now, in this present moment, being made known to us and in us.

My confusion with the words Jesus spoke at the first communion was solved; in fact, it became a breathtaking wonder—the marvelous work that only God the Holy Spirit can accomplish. This is what 1 Corinthians 2 speaks of, when Paul, quoting Isaiah, tells us the Spirit makes the Gospel real to us today:

> "Eye has not seen, nor ear heard, nor have entered into the heart of man the things which God has prepared for those who love Him. But God has revealed them to us through His Spirit. For the Spirit searches all things, yes, the deep things of God…Now we have received, not the spirit of the world, but the Spirit who is from God, that we might know the things that have been freely given to us by God." 1 Corinthians 2:9-12 (NKJV)

In these verses, we see Paul explaining that the Spirit reveals to us all that God has prepared in Christ—and it is by the Spirit that we are present to those gifts in the Eucharist today. Through this revelation, the Eucharist takes on an entirely new wonder! In the Holy Spirit, we are present to the ascended Jesus—present to all He is and all He accomplished; we are intimately present and inside of Him and aware that He is inside of us.

We eat and drink of Him, fully recognizing that He is present within us now.

> "...Is not the cup of blessing which we bless a sharing in the blood of Christ? Is not the bread which we break a sharing in the body of Christ?" 1 Corinthians 10:16

> "The cup of blessing [of wine at the Lord's Supper] upon which we ask [God's] blessing, does it not mean [that in drinking it] we participate in and share a fellowship (a communion) in the blood of Christ (the Messiah)? The bread which we break, does it not mean [that in eating it] we participate in and share a fellowship (a communion) in the body of Christ?" 1 Corinthians 10:16 (AMP)

> "Our co-participation with the blood of Jesus...the bread our co-participation in the body of Christ". In the notes of that verse the Passion gives the Aramaic as "in the presence of His blood...the presence of His body." 1 Corinthians 10:16 (TPT)

We are recognizing and declaring that, in this moment, we are participating in and sharing in all that the blood of Christ means and is now being realized in us. Likewise, we share in the incarnation, acknowledging that we are, in fact, one with Him—

resting in the truth that we are co-crucified, buried, risen, and ascended with Him.

We are ***not striving toward some distant goal, nor are we trying to 'arrive,' or seek some blessing***. We are not saying: "**Please give me**, do this, make me…crucify me, resurrect me, **help** me overcome."

> **We are in this moment, *there*—even as He and all He did is *here, now in an eternal IS***. He is *there* as a fact of history while *simultaneously here* and *now* in our experience.

Every week—or many times a week—we celebrate the reality that He is with us, and in us, in the mundane details of our everyday lives.

Considering the enormity of what is taking place, one would expect it to be a strike of divine power—a knock-you-on-the-floor kind of moment! But it is quiet, mysterious, while Someone is happening at a very deep level.

When we go for an x-ray, we are left sitting alone in front of the machine while the operator stands in a separate room. We hear a click, feel nothing, and see nothing! But if we think nothing happened, we are mistaken. The x-ray silently penetrates our bodies, capturing an image, and if we are exposed to that ray for too long, something bad happens! That is the reason the operator is in a different room when the ray is released.

Week after week, or even daily, as we gather for this sacred Meal, we are reminded that this is not just a routine; it's an extraordinary reality. Every time we partake in the Eucharist, we celebrate the tangible presence of Christ within us and around us, in the seemingly mundane details of our everyday lives. It's not an event that overwhelms with a visible spectacle, but a quiet, mysterious unfolding where, at a deep level, Someone is happening—changing us from the inside out.

6. Christ Incarnate

In remembrance of ***Me****.*

The communion that I grew up with focused exclusively on the sufferings and death of Jesus, often accompanied by sad hymns meant to stir emotions and engage our Western memory. Yet, if we focus on His suffering and death, we must also include His resurrection, ascension, and the giving of the Spirit—for His death holds no value without His resurrection and ascension to the Father.

> *Jesus does not merely accomplish salvation for us—He is salvation! Salvation is the Person of Jesus.*

This leads us to a deeper meaning of "Me." When Jesus says, "Do this in remembrance of Me," He is not referring to a single aspect of His life or death. *Me* encompasses the totality of Jesus Messiah—recognizing Him as the Son of God, co-equal with the

Father and the Spirit. It includes the fact of His union with creation, especially with humanity, a union that arises from His being the Creator of all that exists.

> *Me,* in the body and blood, is the Person of Jesus, confronting us with the incarnation, in which He becomes one with all humanity—dwelling in each of us.
>
> *Me,* is the One who, with humanity, forges a relationship with us at our worst, even as we tortured Him with the intent of killing Him.
>
> *Me,* is the One who took us into Himself at our worst—becoming us, becoming our sin, becoming our curse—and carried all to death.
>
> *Me,* is the One who rose from the dead with His glorified human body, declaring that sin has been lifted away from us and that we are now inside of Him, with Him, face to face with the Father in the Spirit.
>
> *Me,* is the One they knew—the Lover of the outcast, the broken, the Savior from sin.
>
> *Me* is the one who is now with us, in us, at home with us, wherever we find ourselves in life.

Jesus is the Shepherd who has found us and now declares, *"Rejoice with Me, for I have found My sheep!"* Every action of His life was not for Himself, but for us. His obedience, His love, His trust in the Father—all were for our sake. He did not assume our flesh for a private relationship with the Father, nor was He here for His own benefit. Every second of His life, His suffering, death, and resurrection was lived solely for us. He receives the Spirit for us and as us. From eternity, He has lived in the Spirit, and at the Jordan, He received the Spirit, continuing to live in Him and teaching His human flesh to listen and follow the Spirit on our behalf. His compassionate love for all people, inspiring His teaching and the way He healed the sick, was done for us and as us. His obedience and faithfulness to the Father were fully accomplished as our representative.

His life, lived in His incarnate body, was not only for us but as us! Every human being participated in and partook of His life—His blood-shedding, His death, and His resurrection. His life, poured out for us, is infinitely enough. Now we are wrapped in Him, and He in us—*Christ our life, Christ lives in me, Christ in me*—these all speak of the kind of life we now live, drawing our very life from His Person.

Paul captures this profound union when he writes, *"The life I now live in the flesh, I live by the faith of the Son of God, who loved me and gave Himself for me"* Galatians 2:20. This life is not something we can live on our own, nor are we meant to try. Our salvation from sin is Christ living His life through us, walking in union with Him, and in Him, to live in relationship with the Father. Our salvation is the gift of Himself to all mankind!

As we remember, eat, and drink of His Body and Blood, we are not just recalling historical events. We are co-participating in Him—sharing in His resurrected, ascended mind, imagination, feelings, emotions, and body. Paul's realization, *"For me to live is Christ,"* is not just a theological statement, but the heart of the Gospel itself. It exposes as false the insipid religious substitute that presents the Gospel as 'trying to be like Jesus!' The Christian life is *Him in us*.

This is the wonder of the Eucharist! He is here, now, in the fullness of His Person, knowing us completely and intimately. As we participate in Him, He becomes to us exactly what we need, even if we do not yet fully understand what that is. He does not give us a formula or a program—He gives us Himself. We come to Jesus Messiah, the Risen, Ascended Person and receive from Him all that we need Him to be to us.

The Gospel is not about methods or self-improvement; it is about participating in the Person of Jesus through the Spirit. In Him, we are brought to the Father, who loves us as He loves His Son. When we reduce the Gospel to a mere ticket to heaven or a guide to better living, we miss its true, magnificent depth.

7. The Night of All Nights

What happened on that night of all nights?

It was the night of Passover, a celebration of Israel's deliverance from Egypt, yet Jesus transformed its meaning in ways the disciples could scarcely have imagined. Jesus sent some of the disciples to a house with a prearranged house signal, where they could celebrate Passover in private. The betrayer must not know the location, so those sent to prepare were to look for a man carrying a water pot—a most unusual sight, as women typically carried the water pots.

This room was to become a hallowed spot in their memory. It was a room hidden away in the maze of Jerusalem's backstreets. Jesus was excited at the thought of eating Passover with them; He told them He was fulfilling a great desire to spend this special family night with them and had taken time to hide it from the curious crowds so they might be alone together that night.

At this pivotal moment in history, Jesus gave new identity to the familiar Passover bread and wine. With the breaking of the bread, He revealed a new meaning: "This is My body." As He took the third cup of wine, traditionally part of the Passover meal, He transformed it into a declaration of the New Covenant—a new kind of deliverance, one that would lead humanity out of sin and death.

Tonight, He would unpack the gift by which He would be with them through the rest of their lives and be present to untold millions in the centuries to come—a supernatural Meal of remembrance, mystery, and wonder. But this room, filled with joy and family, would also witness the first steps toward His death and resurrection, the salvation of all humanity. For this night, the prophets had waited, not knowing what it would look like. It was the night the cosmos would change, when the powers of darkness holding humanity in chains of lies would be confronted and defeated. On this night, Love gave Himself to save those who rejected and tortured Him.

The Passover meal centered around four cups of wine, marking key moments of the evening. The first two cups represented the historical deliverance from Egypt under Moses. But on this night, Jesus took the third cup and redefined it, proclaiming it as the New Covenant—a new exodus, leading humanity out of the bondage of sin and death.

Each of the Gospel writers gives us a slightly different record of what was said and took place on this night, as the Spirit impressed it on their memory:

"While they were eating, Jesus took some bread, and after a blessing, He broke it and gave it to the disciples, and said, "Take, eat; this is My body." And when He had taken a cup and given thanks, He gave it to them, saying, "Drink from it, all of you; for this is My blood of the covenant, which is poured out for many for the forgiveness of sins. But I say to you, I will not drink this fruit of the vine from now on until that day when I drink it new with you in My Father's kingdom." Matthew 26:26-29

"While they were eating, He took some bread, and after a blessing He broke it, and gave it to them, and said, "Take it; this is My body." And when He had taken a cup and given thanks, He gave it to them, and they all drank from it. And He said to them, "This is My blood of the covenant, which is poured out for many. Truly I say to you, I will never again drink of the fruit of the vine until that day when I drink it new in the kingdom of God." Mark 14:22-25

"When the hour had come, He reclined at the table, and the apostles with Him. And He said to them, "I have earnestly desired to eat this Passover with you

> before I suffer; for I say to you, I shall never again eat it until it is fulfilled in the kingdom of God." And when He had taken a cup and given thanks, He said, "Take this and share it among yourselves; for I say to you, I will not drink of the fruit of the vine from now on until the kingdom of God comes." And when He had taken some bread and given thanks, He broke it and gave it to them, saying, "This is My body which is given for you; do this in remembrance of Me." And in the same way, He took the cup after they had eaten, saying, "This cup which is poured out for you is the new covenant in My blood." Luke 22:14-20

As Jesus said the words, no one looked shocked or leaned forward to interrupt Him with questions. That is remarkable, considering they were constantly vocalizing their ignorance of what He was talking about! In silence, they took the bread and ate it, and likewise, they drank from the cup of wine. The difference between tonight and a year ago in the synagogue in Capernaum!

As young Jews eating Passover, what would they have understood in the words of Jesus? The mystery of eating His flesh and drinking His blood remained, but Jesus wrapped that mystery in words of prophecy that these young men had been raised hearing.

The words *New Covenant* shed much light on the Meal that Jesus was instituting that night.

Jesus was very specific: *"This is My blood of the New Covenant..."* Everyone at the table knew their history, and the prophet Jeremiah had spoken some 500 years earlier about the end of the Mosaic covenant, which would be replaced by the New Covenant.

> ""Behold, days are coming", declares the LORD, "when I will make a new covenant with the house of Israel and with the house of Judah, not like the covenant which I made with their fathers in the day I took them by the hand to bring them out of the land of Egypt, My covenant which they broke, although I was a husband to them," declares the LORD." Jeremiah 31:31-33

The emphasis in Jesus' words was on *new*. In the language of the Bible, *new* can have two meanings. One refers to something simply added to a series—a baby in a long line of human births or a car that follows the last model. But the *new* of the New Covenant was something entirely different—*something never seen before in human history.*

Ancient societies were bound together by the cement of covenants. We find ordinary people making covenants in marriage, in business partnerships, and kings making covenants with lesser kings, making both stronger. It was the way life functioned in those days. Such a covenant had been given to Israel in the early chapters of Exodus, establishing a covenant with God. However, all such covenants were flawed, especially the one between God and Israel, because they depended on trust, the faithfulness of both parties, and their readiness and willingness to keep the promises of the covenant. The covenant made at Mount Sinai was made by the representatives of Israel shouting their willingness to do everything He commanded. If they had truly known themselves and been aware of their limitations, the best they might have said would have been, "We will do our best; we will try hard!"

Their trying hard ended in a broken covenant—maybe 'smashed' would be a better word! They finally said, "Forget it!" With the covenant in shambles, God brought the nation to a halt. Ten of the tribes had gone into captivity to Assyria a number of years earlier; now the two remaining tribes went in chains to Babylon, where they would remain for seventy years. It was during those final months of the tribe of Judah that Jeremiah gave his solemn words, as quoted above. The covenant was broken and finished, making way for a new covenant that would change everything for everyone—a covenant that would depend solely on the faithfulness of God, a covenant that man could not break because God upheld the entire action! It was a new covenant that had not been imagined in anyone's wildest dreams.

Before we turn back through the centuries to examine the roots of the New Covenant, it is imperative that we first understand what a covenant is, and then discover what makes this one the *New* Covenant. Read slowly; to this day this is the only way God deals with mankind.

Religion, with its agenda of false hope, changes the meaning of words to fit their salvation model of 'acceptance by working hard,' subtly turning the word *covenant* into *contract.* These two words stand in stark opposition to one another.

A contract is based on distrust! We hire a person to do a job, but because we do not know him or have solid reason to trust him, a contract is drawn up. A contract describes the job and the promise of the worker to complete it for an agreed-upon price. On the other side of the contract, the payer promises to pay that agreed price once the job is completed. If the work is not done according to the contract, the payer may refuse to pay and even sue the worker. Likewise, if the job is completed as stipulated in the contract, the worker must be paid. If the payment is not made, the worker may sue to receive it.

A contract is a legal document in which someone promises to do something, with specific terms for the work involved, along with the threat of punishment if it is not done or the promise of reward upon its completion.

Religion views its relationship with God as a contract—a transaction in which, if they do their part and keep the rules, if they manage their sin and achieve a state of reasonable morality, they will be rewarded with a place in heaven. If they fail to keep the rules, they will be punished in eternal torment!

A covenant is utterly different.

It arises from trust and the self-giving of both parties, committing themselves to being there for the other and keeping every promise of the covenant they are now making. A covenant was a solemn event, built on a life-and-death oath, sacred faithfulness to one's word. A covenant functioned by faithfulness— trust in the other party's covenant oath, resting in their faithfulness, trusting oneself to the other as a child to his parents. *This is what the New Testament means by belief and believing!*

A covenant is most solemn—an oath made with shed blood of the parties to the covenant, binding them to its promises. The bloodshed was usually a cut in the arm or hand, serving as a declaration that they would be faithful to the covenant, keeping their promises even to the shedding of their own blood, and if necessary, even to death. There was no possibility for one party to abandon the covenant; only death could end it. A covenant breaker would die in accordance with the oath sworn at the making of the covenant!

The blood was shed for the other party to the covenant; it said plainly, *"I love you to the point, if necessary, of giving my life, to the shedding of my blood, to keep my promises to you. If I should fail and abandon you, leaving you to the will of your enemies, I now call upon God to shed my blood, for I failed to be faithful to my word and am not worthy to live."*

A covenant signified the union of two parties in a lifelong, faithful commitment of each one to the other. The word 'righteousness' describes two parties of a covenant, walking together *in sync*, seeing themselves mirrored in their covenant partner.

Every covenant ended in a meal—most of the time consisting of bread and wine—that, with boldness and rejoicing, ratified the covenant, declaring that an inseparable relationship was now in place. *This is the thanksgiving of the Eucharist that we now celebrate, giving thanks that He has finished the work; there is nothing left for us to do!* Yet, it is this truth that multiple thousands of people revolt against and refuse to accept!

A covenant had nothing to do with reward or punishment, but was solely about strong, lifelong love, and mutual trust in each other's faithfulness. In this case, our God—Father, Son, and Holy Spirit—who is divine Love, is not only faithful but also is our faithfulness and strength to be a covenant member.

8. The Everlasting Covenant

The promise God first made to Abram (whom He later renamed Abraham) was given while he was in Ur of Chaldea (early 2000 BC), and was later repeated in Haran:

> "Now the Lord said to Abram, 'Go forth from your country, and from your relatives and from your father's house, to the land which I will show you; and I will make you a great nation, and I will bless you, and make your name great; and so you shall be a blessing; and I will bless those who bless you, and the one who curses you I will curse. And in you all the families of the earth will be blessed.'" Genesis 12:1-3

It was obvious that before Abraham could have enough descendants to become a great nation, he would have to begin with one son—the heir to the promise! The child that Abraham and Sarah were promised, was the key to the prophecy!

At a chaotic time in Abraham's life, the next step was unveiled. By this time both Abraham and Sarah were childless, old, and beyond childbearing age. *The fulfillment of the promise through a son and heir had ceased to be challenging—it had become impossible.* Abraham had even arranged for his trusted servant Eliezer to be named his heir. It was as Abraham mulled over all the blessings of God, except the gift of the all-important son, that God added to the word of promise a covenant, binding Himself to faithfully fulfill His word of giving a son. *He did not need a covenant to be faithful as man does, but He did this for Abraham's sake, and for the sake of his children that would be born to him.*

> "For when God made the promise to Abraham, since He could swear by no one greater, He swore by Himself, saying, 'I will surely bless you and I will surely multiply you.' And so, having patiently waited, he obtained the promise. For men swear by one greater than themselves, and with them an oath given as confirmation is an end of every dispute. In the same way God, desiring even more to show to the heirs of the promise the unchangeableness of His purpose, interposed with an oath, so that by two unchangeable things, in which it is impossible for God to lie, we who have taken refuge

> would have strong encouragement to
> take hold of the hope set before us."
> Hebrews 6:13-18

In the days of Abraham, in the land of Canaan, there was a ritual for making a covenant. We find the record of such a covenant in Genesis 15. Specific animals and birds were taken, and the animals were cut in half. The bloody halves were placed opposite each other, creating a path of blood between them. Then the two parties of the covenant would walk toward each other between the dead birds and bloody pieces of the animals, making a path of bloodshed and death. As each walked toward the other, their feet in the animals' blood, both swore an oath to God upon their own life that they would keep the covenant, even to death. If they failed in their promise, they called for their own death. Meeting in the middle, they would clasp hands or arms—bloody from incisions made in their own bodies, with their blood mingling in the clasp. They were known as *blood brothers,* bound in covenant oath through the shedding of their blood.

This is the first wonder! It was unknown in human history—that God would enter a covenant with a human. The Creator, giving Himself and binding Himself with an oath to the creature! This is the first word of the Gospel—*God will give Himself to His creatures and make a covenant with a human being, with Abraham.* But the wonder is a mystery. Abraham, the one who will receive all the benefits of the covenant, was put into a deep sleep, and in the sleep, he received a vision of what was happening. He was present as the covenant was made; he saw what took place, *but he could not take his part and walk the bloody path, making his promises as one swearing his faithfulness to the covenant.*

As he watched, Abraham saw a recognized symbol of Yahweh—flames and smoke—pass along the bloody path between the pieces of the covenant sacrifice, but Yahweh went alone. *One Person, taking the place of both parties,* made the covenant between Yahweh and Abraham, yet it was made solely by Yahweh in the fiery presence of His glory. The one fiery person moving through the pieces was both Yahweh *and Abraham!*

Abraham was unable to move or take part. He saw and understood the event, but was unable to leave his place to be involved in, or explain, the mystery.

Abraham was to be party to the covenant he never signed, for Yahweh signed it as him! God swore on His own being, elevating the promise He had given to Abraham to covenant status. The promise now was sealed with God's oath; it was unbreakable, backed by His faithfulness and honor. *God swore upon the life of God!*

By taking the place of both parties, Yahweh—signing His own name as the sole covenant maker and keeper—was declaring that if either He or Abraham failed to keep the covenant, God would take the death upon Himself! ***Abraham could not break the covenant because he never signed it with his own blood and oath.*** His only part was to see and grasp what this meant and to trust himself to the God who made and guaranteed the covenant. Jesus referred to this revelation Abraham had when He said, "Your father Abraham rejoiced to see My day, and he saw it and was glad" John 8:56.

As Abraham slept, he saw the symbol of Yahweh—fire and smoke–moving through the pieces, alone on the path of covenant blood and death. Yahweh was making a covenant in His own name *and in the name of Abraham*, not doing this *for* Abraham but *as* him! Abraham made no promises, nor did he swear his readiness to die to keep covenant promises. He rested in sleep as God took upon Himself full responsibility, not only for His own part in keeping the covenant, but also for *Abraham's part in keeping the covenant.* God took the place of both Himself and mankind.

Our trust is in Him who exercised His faith *as us*. The Eucharist is not to ask for forgiveness but to rejoice that God kept His word in the blood of Jesus. *We* have been cleansed, washed in the blood of the Lamb and have overcome all the forces of evil. *We* are not in the covenant because we had enough faith, but because we rest helplessly in Him who *brought us through with His faith!* We are not 'in' because we saw clearly what took place in His sufferings and death, but because "He saw for and as us and interprets His mind to us through the Spirit" 1 Corinthians 2:10-11.

We do not struggle to come to Him with our pathetic spoonful of natural faith. Instead, we are awakened, and eyes are opened to see who and what we have. In that moment, we give thanks—not asking for forgiveness, but thanking Him for freely giving it to us.

God swore the covenant oath, meaning that if He failed to keep His word, then God would die, and all creation dissolve into nothingness with Him! He does all He does, *'for His Name's sake!'* Nothing is done for our name's sake, for we do not swear the oath. Our salvation rests on His faithfulness to His promise *and that alone.*

Faith is not an inner energy that enables one to make something happen, but *eyes open to see that it has happened,* and all that remains is to rejoice with thanksgiving.

Religion builds its salvation on continually telling us that we are unworthy, unwanted, unlovable, and that we must make ourselves worthy, lovable, and wanted before we could even consider God making a move toward us!

If you have doubts and lingering fears of having unforgiven sin, it is because at this moment, you are believing that your salvation hangs on your attempts to repent and believe, rather than resting in His insight and faith that has sworn upon His own life blood to be your Savior moment by moment. This is how this life in Christ begins and continues in rest—as we begin, so we continue.

But a faulty beginning leads to a life filled with the struggle of trying to make the right promise to God, offering ourselves as the guarantee! We live with religious anxiety, constantly trying to imitate Jesus and measuring our growth by what we have accomplished in order to advance in religion's idea of walking with God.

> *Come to partake of His body and blood with no promise on your lips, only giving thanks!*

We cannot break the covenant any more than we can earn or deserve it, for we did not sign it in our own blood, nor were we there to swear to keep the promises! He was alone, standing as each one of us, swearing His oath upon Himself to save and keep us to the end.

John and Paul lay it out very bluntly:

> *"We love because He first loved us!" 1 John 4:19*
>
> *"Not that we loved God but that He loved us…" 1 John 4:10*
>
> *"While we were yet sinners, Christ died for us." Romans 5:8*

First, we are engulfed with His love and then we find our response—trust and rest in the knowledge that we are loved where and as we are, without lifting a finger. God loves us, not because of who we are or what we have done, but because of who He eternally is.

We did not perform some great work to be admitted into the kingdom of God. Rather, through the Spirit, He awakened us to realize His love for us, to see that the celebration is already in full swing, and to know we are called to take our place as much-loved children of God. The party of rejoicing is a gift out of the heart of the Trinity, with no door charge—all is free!

> The goal of the covenant was the fulfillment of the Trinity's intention in creating mankind.

From before the beginning, man was created to be in Christ, the incarnate Son of God, face to face with the Father, endued with the Spirit. From this relationship, men and women would partake of the same relationship, the same love that was eternally known between Father and Son in the Holy Spirit—the same divine peace, joy, wisdom, and strength. This was mankind's nature; it was as natural for mankind to be in this dynamic relationship with the Trinity as it was for Christ to know Himself as one with the Father inside His infinite love.

> Mankind was to rule the creation as vice-regent of the Creator.

The man's mind was darkened by the Satanic lie that introduced the darkness—that man was separated from God, alone and lost in a terrible dementia, forgetting who he was created to be. He wandered into the death-ruled world of the Satanic lie, tasting all its fears and exploring every dead-end path in that terrifying darkness. The Lie promised man could be an independent god, operating separately outside of the One true God, breaking the relationship with God (at least in his own mind) for which he was created. Mankind listened to the enticing word, tasted the false freedom it offered, stepped off the path, and was lost, In the profound darkness of Satanic deceit, man could no longer remember the character of the true God or his own identity as one created to be a son of that God! The Lie plunged mankind into confusion, spiritual dementia, a profound darkness—mere existence in a state of death. This death brought the unshakeable belief that he was separated from God, abandoned, and unloved. It brought futility in everything he touched.

But God, in love, would not be governed by mankind's action. God Himself sent God the Son—God from God—to become one with mankind. He took to Himself the flesh and nature of man without ceasing to be God, not merely as a rescue operation to find lost humans who had forgotten who they were, but infinitely more—to rescue man and restore every man and woman to the original blueprint of being made in the image and likeness of God! In the humiliation of the Son becoming human, every person would be joined to Him, participate in His divine nature, and be exalted to the high position for which they were created. Adam's being lost in the darkness was a diversion, but one that revealed the love of the Trinity to be infinitely greater than anyone could have imagined.

The purpose of the Trinity—Father, Son, and Holy Spirit—determined that the Son of God, co-equal with the Father and the Spirit, would come and bring every man and woman, all families of the earth, to resurrection and participation in the intention behind creation.

This covenant, uniting God and man face to face in love, was carried out in Jesus Christ. It is vitally important to know that this covenant did not exist in isolation; its roots trace back to the Trinity's Everlasting Covenant with each other before time, but it was fleshed out in time through Abraham and the covenant God made with him (see Genesis 15), and came to fulfillment in Jesus, who is designated the Seed or Descendant of Abraham.

Abraham's faith in God found its final rest in the covenant. "Abraham believed God, and it was counted to him for righteousness" Genesis 15:6. This phrase encompasses his faith that began in Ur with the hearing of the first promise and is now sealed with the covenant oath on God's part.

He did not have to perform some great good deed to be called righteous—he simply trusted the God who would keep His word in due time. The phrase *'counted to him'* is a mathematician's term, meaning that placing his trust in the God who was faithful adds up to righteousness. Righteousness is a relational word, having nothing to do with the piling up of good works! It does not mean that Jesus lived doing righteous things that are mysteriously credited to your account! It means having and experiencing a relationship of being face to face with the Other—seeing oneself in the Covenant Partner, seeing one's image in the Other, which is exactly what happened: He as us, we as Him!

The promise at the heart of this covenant was that in Abraham and his Seed or Descendant, all families of the earth would be blessed. This promise is later picked up in the covenant with David.

The covenant of Law made in Exodus with Moses as mediator could not change the covenant with Abraham, made nearly 500 years earlier, which required no work by Abraham—only his trust, resting into the faithfulness of God.

In Jerusalem, 600 years after Jeremiah introduced hope of the New Covenant, Jesus, in the upper room, on the rooftop, eating Passover and conversing with His disciples, introduced the New Covenant Meal of bread and wine, announcing that Jeremiah's prophetic word was finally coming to pass. He called it '*the* New Covenant in My blood'—He did not call it just another covenant! This covenant has been waiting through the centuries to be fulfilled, and tonight was the night.

The New Covenant, the covenant of all covenants, also called the Everlasting Covenant—the covenant that spans from before time in the counsel of the Trinity—it is here, now in this moment, and to the ages beyond our time space moment. But '*everlasting*' never refers to 'heaven when we die!' It comes from the heart of the Trinity, *never to come to an end* as the Mosaic covenant did, *but it is always here and now in all its fullness!*

As we saw earlier, in the Greek language of the New Testament, the word *new* describing the New Covenant means new in kind—something never seen before, beyond the thinking of this moment but present with us now. This covenant had never been seen before, never imagined, and could only be revealed by the Spirit.

> "Yet we do speak wisdom among those who are mature; a wisdom, however, not of this age nor of the rulers of this age, who are passing away; but we speak God's wisdom in a mystery, the hidden *wisdom* which God predestined before the ages to our glory; *the wisdom* which none of the rulers of this age has understood; for if they had understood it, they would not have crucified the Lord of glory; but just as it is written, "THINGS WHICH EYE HAS NOT SEEN AND EAR HAS NOT HEARD, AND *which* HAVE NOT ENTERED THE HEART OF MAN, ALL THAT GOD HAS PREPARED FOR THOSE WHO LOVE HIM." For to us God revealed them through

> the Spirit; for the Spirit searches all things, even the depths of God." 1 Corinthians 2:6-10

A *New* Covenant, such as they had never seen or imagined in their wildest dreams, was now ushered in by the Spirit, declared in this Meal of mystery and wonder, nourishing us with the true food from beyond time and space. We can say with Jesus, "I have meat to eat that you know not of!" Those at the table that night were the first of myriads of persons to participate in eating the body and drinking the blood of the Covenant Maker, walking as persons of light in a life that eye has not seen, nor ear heard, neither has it entered into the heart of man—what God has prepared for those who love Him. But now the mystery has cleared, and we see, hear, and can imagine the wonder revealed to us by the Spirit.

The covenant with Abraham was further spelled out in the writings of Jeremiah and Ezekiel. The prophets called it the *New* Covenant because the Mosaic Law had taken center stage as the standard of what man must do to achieve righteousness, but it had come to its end, failing to make man righteous, leaving him condemned and lost. *The people had missed the meaning of the earlier covenant with Abraham, in which Yahweh fulfilled the covenant in Himself while mankind was meant to watch and give thanks.* From the beginning, the covenant was a gift, with its final focus on the Seed (or Descendant) of Abraham, which was Jesus. The Law, which could only condemn and judge, was ready to be over and shredded!

Jeremiah spoke of the New Covenant, also calling it the Everlasting Covenant, which would end the Law and set mankind free from its condemnation, guilt, and darkness that came with its breaking.

> "For this is the covenant I will make with the house of Israel after those days," declares the LORD: "I will put My law within them and write it on their heart; and I will be their God, and they shall be My people. They will not teach again, each one his neighbor and each one his brother, saying, 'Know the LORD,' for they will all know Me, from the least of them to the greatest of them," declares the LORD, "for I will forgive their wrongdoing, and their sin I will no longer remember." Jeremiah 31:33-34

The covenant of the Law, upon which the nation was founded, has now collapsed in total failure. *The New Covenant, unlike Moses' covenant written on stone, would now be written within, on our hearts, a principle of new life—the union of God's heart with the human.* This union described the destiny of every man, woman, and child, set forth in the eternal counsel of the Trinity—no separation between God and man.

> "They shall be My people, and I will be their God; and I will give them one heart and one way, so that they may fear Me always, for their own good and for *the good* of their children after them.

> I will make an everlasting covenant with them, that I will not turn away from them, to do them good; and I will put the fear of Me in their hearts so that they will not turn away from Me. I will rejoice over them to do them good, and I will faithfully plant them in this land with all My heart and with all My soul." Jeremiah 32:38-41

'I will put the *fear* of Me in their hearts.' This Old English word 'fear' has nothing to do with being afraid or terrified. It means *to worship, honor, exalt, and even delight in.* Jeremiah expands on this:

> "Behold, I will bring to it health and healing, and I will heal them; and I will reveal to them an abundance of peace and truth… And I will cleanse them from all their iniquity by which they have sinned against Me…. And it shall be to Me a name of joy, praise, and glory before all the nations of the earth, which shall hear of all the good that I do for them, and they shall fear and tremble because of all the good and all the peace that I make for it." Jeremiah 33:6-9

> "Behold, I will do something new, Now it will spring forth; Will you not be aware of it? I will even make a roadway in the wilderness, Rivers in the desert." Isaiah 43:19

> "Behold, days are coming,' declares the Lord,' when I will fulfill the good word which I have spoken concerning the house of Israel and the house of Judah. In those days and at that time I will cause a righteous Branch of David to spring forth; and He shall execute justice and righteousness on the earth. In those days Judah will be saved, and Jerusalem will dwell in safety; and this is *the name* by which she shall be called: the Lord is our righteousness." Jeremiah 33:14-16

The Messiah will be called the Branch—a reference to Isaiah 11, which speaks of the branch growing from the shambles of the root of David. It was also strangely fulfilled in that He was known as 'of Nazareth,' meaning 'the village of the Branch.'

> "I will sprinkle clean water on you, and you will be clean; I will cleanse you from all your filthiness and from all your idols. Moreover, I will give you a new heart and put a new spirit within you; and I will remove the heart of stone from your flesh and give you a heart of flesh. I will put My Spirit within you and cause you to walk in My statutes, and you will be careful to observe My ordinances. You will live in the land that I gave to your forefathers; so you will be My people, and I will be your God." Ezekiel 36:25-28

Galatians tells us that the One in whom the covenant and its promises found fulfillment is the Seed, the descendant of Abraham—Jesus, Son of God, Son of Mary. The coming Messiah was spoken of as the Son of David, and the genealogies found at the beginning of Matthew and Luke show that Jesus is the direct descendant of Abraham through David. Jesus is the promised Seed, the Descendant of Abraham, and the fulfillment of that covenant. As Paul writes in Galatians:

> "Even so, Abraham believed God, and it was reckoned to Him as righteousness. Therefore, be sure that it is those who are of faith who are sons of Abraham. The Scripture, foreseeing that God would justify the Gentiles by faith, preached the gospel beforehand to Abraham, saying, 'all the nations will be blessed in you.' So then those who are of faith are blessed with Abraham, the believe… Christ redeemed us from the curse of the Law, having become a curse for us-for it is written, 'cursed is everyone who hangs on a tree' — in order that in Christ Jesus the blessing of Abraham might come to the Gentiles, so that we would receive the promise of the Spirit through faith.
>
> Brethren, I speak in terms of human relations: even though it is only a man's covenant, yet when it has been ratified, no one sets it aside or adds conditions to it. Now the promises were spoken to Abraham and to his seed. He does not

say, 'And to seeds,' as referring to many, but rather to one, 'And to your seed,' that is, Christ. What I am saying is this: the Law, which came four hundred and thirty years later, does not invalidate a covenant previously ratified by God, so as to nullify the promise. For if the inheritance is based on law, it is no longer based on a promise; but God has granted it to Abraham by means of a promise…

For you are all sons of God through faith in Christ Jesus. For all of you who were baptized into Christ have clothed yourselves with Christ. There is neither Jew nor Greek, there is neither slave nor free man, there is neither male nor female; for you are all one in Christ Jesus. And if you belong to Christ, then you are Abraham's descendants, heirs according to promise…

But when the fullness of the time came, God sent forth His Son, born of a woman, born under the Law, so that He might redeem those who were under the Law, that we might receive the adoption as sons. Because you are sons, God has sent forth the Spirit of His Son into our hearts, crying, 'Abba! Father!' Therefore, you are no longer a slave, but a son, and if a son, then an heir through God." Galatians 3:6-4:7

The first miracle of Jesus points us to a similar yet different wonder. Hidden from the eyes of the wedding guests, in the kitchen, Jesus had the servants fill six large pots with 180 gallons of water—they knew it was water! They had filled the pots themselves! Jesus silently speaking within Himself to the water in the pots, knew it had become the most uncommon water in the hill country of Galilee! He told the servants to now pour what they knew was water into containers and serve it to the V.I.P.s at the wedding party, *as wine!* How could one describe what went through their minds? They knew it was water, yet trusted Him and His word; they acted as if it were wine, and in the pouring, red wine flowed into the container! The water had *become something else* showing forth His glory! It was one of the quietest wonders Jesus performed. Something of the same kind happens as we do as He commanded, to eat and drink of Him.

> "Great are the works of the LORD; they are studied by all who delight in them. Splendid and majestic is His work, and His righteousness endures forever. He has made His wonders to be remembered; the LORD is gracious and compassionate. He has given food to those who fear Him; He will remember His covenant forever." Psalm 111:2-5

The difference with what He did that night of Passover was that *He did not turn the bread and wine into something else but declared it to be the very presence of His own true self!*

9. Eucharist Language

What is often overlooked is that what began in Capernaum a year earlier is now completed, and what He had said before is now given as the way in which it will be carried out. In Capernaum, He had said that we are to eat His flesh and drink His blood; now in Jerusalem, He incorporates into the Passover meal the New Meal of His flesh and blood, taking bread and wine and declaring, *"...this is My body given for you" and "My blood of the new covenant shed for you and for many for the forgiveness of sins."*

Immediately after, He gave the meandering discourse—one of the longest that we have recorded of His recorded words. In grasping what He was saying, we must remember that it followed the introduction of the New Covenant Meal, the Eucharist, and the discourse of the previous year explains this one. The key words from the Capernaum discourse are found throughout this one in the rooftop room in Jerusalem. Interestingly, the previous discourse calling for the eating of His flesh and drinking of His blood is also one of His longest recorded teachings. I find it fascinating that two of the longest communications of Jesus are both entirely centered on the New Covenant Meal, the Eucharist!

The first time, a year earlier, His words caused outrage, and the congregation walked out. This time, when He speaks again of eating His flesh, or body, and drinking His blood, it is received in accepting silence. The disciples do not understand; Jesus tells them they will not until the Spirit comes. Yet, they receive His words in complete trust, and they will teach their disciples, word for word, what Jesus said. As a result, this Meal will be celebrated over the next 2,000 years using the same words that Jesus taught them that night.

He begins to speak of the focus of His entire ministry: "In My Father's house are many abiding places; if it were not so, I would have told you" John 14:2. In the first days of His ministry, He referred to the Temple as being the physical pointer on earth of His Father's House in the heavens (see John 2:19). In that true, invisible House, there are limitless abiding places.

In the Old Testament, the psalms of David referred to *'the House of the LORD,'* declaring that he would dwell in it forever (see Psalm 23:6, 27:4), even though he wrote this before the Temple had been built! David was clearly referring to *an invisible, ever present, yet very real dwelling of God,* where he lived his life in close relationship with Him every day. It was a place that provided shelter and security in the day of trouble. He also speaks of Yahweh as being his refuge—a secure high place of safety, a secret place of revelation and insight into the ways of God.

This was not his imagination! Dreams and imagination cannot deflect spears or save him from his enemies!

> "Do you not know? Have you not heard?
> The Everlasting God, the LORD, the Creator of the ends of the earth does not become weary or tired. His understanding is inscrutable. He gives strength to the weary, and to him who lacks might He increases power. Though youths grow weary and tired, and vigorous young men stumble badly, yet those who wait for the LORD will gain new strength; they will mount up with wings like eagles, they will run and not get tired, they will walk and not become weary."
> Isaiah 40:28-31

The Hebrew word we translate as 'wait' is a picture word, describing being platted, or braided together. Our fragile, weak human strength is *braided with His unlimited strength,* so that our *weakness is swallowed in His strength and His strength becomes our strength!* The phrase '*gain new strength*' could be better translated as '*they exchange strengths*!' Our weakness and inability are *exchanged for His strength, ability, and power.*

In the Incarnation, God the Son becomes flesh and lives in the Trinity love relationship with the Father, listening to Him through every day and being kept safe within Him. He brings His hiding place, His abiding place in the Father's love, to all so that we may share and know the Father as He does! The Holy Spirit makes this relationship–the place of peace, joy, and safety—real to humankind. Jesus assures them that there is plenty of room in this invisible home, the place of rest while we live in this world, pressured by darkness, dangers, and enemies.

Our confusion began with the wrong translation of 'abiding places,' substituting 'mansion' instead. From that mistake has arisen every twisted image of heaven; with the help of Hollywood, it has been interpreted as a physical mansion made of brick, cement, and stone with gold trim. In such an interpretation which has guided some sections of the church for decades, there is no reference to the Father, Son or Holy Spirit; we live *forever and ever,'* fulfilling our envious dreams of the rich and famous!

The word should have been translated as 'abiding places'; Jesus used the same root word in the Greek a few minutes later in John 15 when He said, *"Abide in Me and I in you…"* This makes so much more sense. He is assuring us that in the dwelling place of God the Father, in the heart of God, there is room in Christ for limitless multitudes to live in the closest relationship, face to face with the Christ and the Father. It fulfills Jesus' desire to have us where He is, beholding Him in the glory His Father bestows upon Him. As the conversation in the rooftop room in Jerusalem unfolds, this is referred to as being *in(side)* Christ, *in(side)* the Father.

> "In My Father's house are many abiding places; if it were not so, I would have told you; for I go to prepare a place for you. If I go and prepare a place for you, I will come again and receive you to Myself, *that where I am, there you may be*

> *also*. And you know the way where I am going." John 14:2-4

> *"The glory which You have given Me I have given to them, that they may be one, just as We are one; I in them and You in Me, that they may be perfected in unity, so that the world may know that You sent Me, and loved them, even as You have loved Me. Father*, I desire that they also, whom You have given Me, be with Me where I am, so that they may see My glory which You have given Me, *for You loved Me before the foundation of the world.* O righteous Father, although the world has not known You, yet I have known You; and these have known that You sent Me; and I have made Your name known to them, and will make it known, *so that the love with which You loved Me may be in them, and I in them."* John 17:22-26

The other mistake that has kept multitudes from life in Christ is placing all this on the other side of death. Missing the finished work of Christ, they have interpreted His going away and returning as reference to the second coming. Bible publishers have even inserted headings above many of these verses, offering their opinion that this refers to the believer's future glory! However, these verses refer to His going away in death, through the cross, which would culminate with His return *in the resurrection* and the *giving of the Spirit,* and believers would be called those who are seated in heavenly places—now!

His words, *'If it were not so, I would have told you,'* indicate that this has been the burden of all He has said to them; this is not an add-on to His main teaching but the very heart of it. *It means we can say with authority that the focus of His coming was to bring us into intimate heart knowing, dwelling with the Father.*

The expression used here and throughout the remainder of the New Testament—*'in Christ'* and *'Christ in you,'*—describes the seamless, inseparable union that exists between the believer and Christ, and this is extended to include God the Father!

In the conversation in Capernaum in John 6, He had used relational expressions that He now expands upon as He passes *His body and blood* to the twelve young men with Him at the table.

Compare these verses:

> "Truly, truly, I say to you, he who believes has *eternal life*. I am the *bread of life.* Your fathers ate the manna in the wilderness, and they died. This is the bread which comes down out of heaven, so that one *may eat it and not die. I am the living bread* that came down out of heaven; if anyone eats of this bread, he will *live forever*; and the *bread also which I will give for the life of the world is My flesh.*" John 6:47-51
>
> So, Jesus said to them, "Truly, truly, I say to you, *unless you eat the flesh of the Son of*

> *Man and drink His blood, you have no life in yourselves. He who eats My flesh and drinks My blood has eternal life, and I will raise him up on the last day. For My flesh is true food, and My blood is true drink. He who eats My flesh and drinks My blood abides in Me, and I in him.* John 6:53-56

Now He uses the same expressions in chapters 14-17, shaping the language of the remainder of the New Testament!

> "Just as the Father has loved Me, I have also loved you; *abide* in My love." John 15:9

> "...that they may all be one*; even as You, Father, are in Me and I in You, that they also may be in Us*, so that the world may believe that You sent Me." John 17:21

> "Jesus said, "Abide in Me, and I in you. As the branch cannot bear fruit of itself unless it abides in the vine, so *neither can you unless you abide in Me. I am the vine, you are the branches; he who abides in Me and I in him*, he bears much fruit, for apart from Me you can do nothing." John 15:4,5

In the words that follow, He introduces not only a *new way of life*, but also the *new language of the New Covenant*. This language had never been known before! It was an entirely new way of understanding oneself, a new way of speaking and understanding this life, revealing hidden mysteries. From henceforth, we have a new identity and must understand ourselves as 'in Christ,' and 'Christ is in me.' Christ in us—*in* perfectly reveals the mysterious relationship brought into being by eating His flesh and drinking His blood. Christ, in the totality of His person, is in us participating in our life, and we, in our humanity, are participating in His risen ascended life. This is the life encapsulated in 'in Christ,' 'Christ in us,' and 'Jesus is the Life, the eternal life.' The Meal perfectly unites these expressions. Eating and drinking of Him speak of seamless union with Him—two inseparable lives lived as one: *'Abide in Me as I abide in you.'* All of this speaks of life *here and now, in this present moment,* and carries no suggestion of waiting until heaven to experience it!

Though the union is seamless—*in*—the two parties do not lose themselves in each other. Christ does not become the believer nor does the believer become Christ. The person who dismisses all their work and service as "It was not me, it was the Lord!" need to mature in understanding. It was indeed *you!* You did not lose yourself in Him nor did He lose Himself in 'you.'" You are two who are one—two delights in one seamless union, able to hold conversation together and work together, something impossible if you have disappeared into Him!

> "After a little while, the world will no longer see Me, but *you will see Me; because I live, you will live also. On that day, you will know that I am in My Father, and you in Me, and I in you*. He who has My commandments and keeps them is the one who loves Me; and he who loves Me will be loved by My Father, and I will love him and will disclose Myself to him." Judas (not Iscariot), said to Him, "Lord, what then has happened that You are going to disclose Yourself to us and not to the world?" Jesus

> answered and said to him, "If anyone loves Me, he will keep My word; and *My Father will love him, and We will come to him and make Our abode with him.*" John 14:19-23

These verses are descriptive, not prescriptive. They describe the person loved by the Father as the one who loves Jesus and keeps His word. It is not a prescription for earning the Father's love, as though the person who loves Jesus will be rewarded with the love of the Father!

> "By this, the love of God was manifested in us, that God has sent His only begotten Son into the world so that we might live through Him. In this is love, *not that we loved God, but that He loved us* and sent His Son to be the propitiation for our sins." 1 John 4:9-10

> "*Love is not defined by our love for God, but by His love for us*. It is not our response to God that attracts His attention; we have always had His undivided affection…" 1 John 4:10 (Mirror Translation)

> "*We love, because He first loved us.*" 1 John 4:19

At the center, this Life, is about humans participating in the love shared within the Trinity.

> "In the unfolding of this day, you will know that we are in seamless union with one another. I am in My Father, you are in Me and I am in you." John 14:20 (Mirror Translation)

The Incarnation makes known to us that we—every man, woman, and child—have been redeemed into inclusion, to participate in the Father, our being in Christ, and the Spirit in us. The Trinity is not broken or disrupted because of our inclusion; rather we are brought in through Christ to partake of Their life, joy, and peace. They delight in us and rejoice with us in everlasting joy. We are joined in inseparable oneness, beloved in infinite intimacy!

God's wondrous intention and blueprint for mankind to live in seamless union with the Father in Christ *has been true since before the foundation of the world!* It is revealed in the finished work of Christ, made known through the Holy Spirit, and discovered by us in the preaching of the Gospel, and every time we celebrate the Eucharist, feasting in the light of this wonder.

This does not mean this intimate relationship comes into existence when we discover it. Gold does not become valuable when I discover it! However, having found it, I now begin to live at the level of wealth my newfound gold has brought to me.

Jesus had shared this in John 14 as they sat at the rooftop table, with crumbs of the bread and the cup of wine, now only with just the dregs left in it, and His words still lingering in their ears:

"This is My body…this is My blood of the new covenant…." Suddenly, He stopped speaking and urgently said, *"Get up, let us go from here"* John 14:31.

The disciples were confused. Passover was not yet finished; another cup still full of wine remained to be drunk, bringing the Passover to conclusion.

As they walk through the streets of Jerusalem under the midnight Passover moon, Jesus continued describing the goal of His mission.

> "I am the true vine, and My Father is the vinedresser. Every branch in Me that does not bear fruit, He takes away; and every branch that bears fruit, He prunes it so that it may bear more fruit. You are already clean because of the words which I have spoken to you. *Abide in Me, and I in you.* As the branch cannot bear fruit of itself unless it abides in the vine, so neither can you unless you abide in Me. I am the vine, you are the branches; *he who abides in Me and I in him, he bears much fruit, for apart from Me you can do nothing."* John 15:1-5

Anyone involved in growing grapes will tell you that the vine has no trunk like a tree, *the vine is the branches!* The vine consists of branches that constitute the vine. Both collectively and individually share in the common sap of the vine, receiving the care and nurture of the farmer. What Jesus is saying is staggering: we are not down here in the world trying to live like Jesus, nor are we getting a religious migraine trying to figure out *what would Jesus do*. He is in us and we in Him, making us one. The Father watches over and cares for us, as *the one vine. Just as the Father cares for Jesus, He is simultaneously caring for us*! He loves us with the same love He has for Jesus because we are, in fact, inseparably one with Jesus! Together we bring forth fruit—divine love in and through our human lives.

The life we live in the home, our school, our work, our little moments of happinesses, despair, and darkness, we are one with Him, and He is with us, so that we spontaneously live Him. *Spontaneous* means we do not need to call a prayer meeting to seek the will of God; we live from within, where the will of God already lives—from the voice of the Father. We produce the fruit of love in action—which we produce from Him who is our life—not He without us, or we without Him, but in the giddy, glorious wonder of He in us.

> "*The glory which You have given Me I have given to them, that they may be one, just as We are one; I in them and You in Me, that they may be perfected in unity, so that the world may know that You sent Me, and loved them, even as You have loved Me. Father*, I desire that they also, whom You have given Me, be with Me where I am, so that they may see My glory which You have given Me, *for You loved Me before the foundation of the world*. O righteous Father, although the world has not known

> You, yet I have known You; and these have known that You sent Me; and I have made Your name known to them, and will make it known, *so that the love with which You loved Me may be in them, and I in them."* John 17:22-26

Remember, He spoke these words immediately after He gave them His body and blood to eat and drink. Eating and drinking go *into* the body and, in this case, fill us with joy as we consume Him, knowing He dwells within us and we live a life united with Him.

The Vine lives in the attention and the loving care of the Father, with Jesus drawing His life from Him. The branches, too, draw life from Christ the vine, and therefore from the Father. Everything the Father is to Christ the vine, He is to the branches, for they are in Christ!

10. The Four Cups

A surface reading of the first Eucharist shows that it is the fulfillment of the Passover meal. As we plunge into the events of that transformative Passover night when Jesus instituted the Eucharist, it's essential to highlight the differences between the Jewish Passover and the Eucharist—the Meal of the New Covenant established by Jesus. Understanding these distinctions is crucial, as it illuminates the deeper significance of the Eucharist. This chapter will guide us through the entire narrative of His sufferings and death, preparing us for deep truths that might otherwise go unnoticed. Ultimately, this chapter is the key to grasping the essence of the Eucharist.

First, let's consider the significance of the Eucharist being instituted during Passover. Importantly, Passover is not tied to the Law. Jesus could have chosen to suffer, die, and establish the Eucharist at any of the Jewish feasts—be it Pentecost, the Day of Atonement, or another. Yet, He selected the one feast that stands apart from the Law.

Passover is the annual celebration of and giving thanks to God for the Exodus—the deliverance from slavery to the Egyptians. The giving of the Law, which occurred approximately three months later at Sinai, was a separate event.

Furthermore, the Passover is connected to the covenant with Abraham not the covenant given to Moses at Sinai. While the Law commands, *'Do this and you will live,'* the promise to Abraham reveals a God of grace who says, *"I will do this for you; trust Me, and therein lies your righteousness and relationship with Me."*

The Passover was a feast for the nation, with lambs sacrificed in the Temple, but also a meal for every family in Israel. On that original night of deliverance, the families of Israel gathered in their slave hovels for this meal. If a person had no family, or if a family was too small to consume the lamb in this one meal, they would join another family. This was not a meal for the independent, isolated loner, but the meal of no separation—one with their God, Yahweh, and one with their kin folk, and fellow Israelites. They would leave Egypt, not only *under the blood* of the lamb, *but with a lamb inside every family unit!*

The way the Meal was eaten remained essentially the same over the centuries since that original night of miracle, but only on the first Passover did they leave the table to join the vast multitude of slaves moving out through the land of Goshen, where the slaves had lived, on the desert road that led to Sinai. It was a meal of remembrance, meaning the deliverance was experienced each time they gathered to eat the meal.

The meal was anchored to a specific form by four cups of wine, mixed with small amounts of water. Each cup moved them through the feast to the finale of giving thanks and praise to God. They were this day, the people of the God—who is their Deliverer—throughout all history. We will quickly go through the meal according to the cups, without going into details of the meal.

The large table was where the family would recline, a symbol of their freedom. As slaves, they had never reclined, but stood, fearfully alert to what the master needed. Each person half-sat, and half-leaned back in a position of complete rest, eating as the free man or woman that they knew themselves to be.

The first cup of wine was brought to the table, along with what today we might call appetizers— bitter herbs to remember the bitterness of slavery. The roasted lamb was set in the center of the table, and it must be consumed by all at this table tonight! By the time of Jesus, the lamb was called *'the body.'* We can find no apparent reason for this, but it is of great significance. This first cup of wine was called the 'cup of sanctification' declaring they were not only a free people, but free as Yahweh's own people.

The second cup of wine was called the 'cup of proclamation.' At this point in the meal, the youngest child would ask *"Why is this night different from all other nights?"* The child would then show how the menus changed throughout the year, but this night never did. The father would then begin telling the history of Israel, based on Deuteronomy 26:

> "You shall answer and say before the Lord
> your God, 'My father was a wandering

> Aramean, and he went down to Egypt
> and sojourned there, few in number;
> but there he became a great, mighty
> and populous nation. And the Egyptians treated us harshly and afflicted us
> and imposed hard labor on us. Then
> we cried to the Lord, the God of our
> fathers, and the Lord heard our voice
> and saw our affliction and our toil and
> our oppression; and the Lord brought
> us out of Egypt with a mighty hand
> and an outstretched arm and with
> great terror and with signs and
> wonders; and He has brought us to this
> place and has given us this land, a land
> flowing with milk and honey."
> Deuteronomy 26:5-9

Within the telling of the story, there would be explanations. As noted above, it was a 'meal of remembrance,' and so the father, followed by all at the table, would declare that *they* were delivered out of Egypt this night, and that *they* were those emancipated from slavery—therefore all should give praise to God, who had *delivered each one of those gathered around this table.*

At this time, the bread was broken, and the meal of roast lamb began. It was at this time, Jesus changed the words and as He broke the bread. He said, *"This is My body given for you,"* In saying, "My body", He not only referenced Himself, but also identified with the lamb they were about to eat, which, as you recall, was called 'the body.'

The third cup of wine, called the 'cup of blessing,' was served after the supper was complete. Jesus defined it as *"This is My blood of the New Covenant, shed for you and for many, for the forgiveness of sins."* He went on to say that He would not drink the wine, until He drank it celebrating that the kingdom of God had come. Confusion!—there is still a fourth cup of wine on the table, waiting for the finale of the feast, which everyone must drink.

Jesus began a conversation outlining life in the New Covenant—a life of union with Himself, of knowing the Father, and the arrival of the Spirit after His departure, who would teach them all things of the New Covenant that He could not teach them at this point. He said the kingdom of God would come when He drank of wine with them, and this is explained in Romans 14 as being like all He had to say in John chapters 14-17: *The kingdom of God is righteousness, peace, and joy in the Holy Spirit.*

They sang the Hallel, Psalms 115-118, and moved directly to the fourth cup, which was the 'cup of praise,' summing up the mood and message of the entire meal. But tonight, after singing the Hallel, Jesus said, "Get up, and let us go out from here!" The disciples, stunned, looked at the fourth cup. Jesus, already on His feet, tells them to join Him. He had not drunk the fourth cup, leaving the meal unfinished, incomplete.

They continued the conversation on the street, as they left the city, following the path to the bridge over the Kidron, leading into the Garden of Gethsemane. He moves into a separate part of the Garden and begins to pray in agony, to the point that blood fills his sweat and runs down His face into His beard. His agony was expressed in a sentence, "If it be possible, let *this cup* pass from Me."

Remember, His agony and praying centered on a specific cup. We must take into consideration that, just moments ago, they had hurriedly left the table in Jerusalem, leaving a cup untouched. Along with that, He announced that He would not drink wine until the kingdom of God had come. He is now speaking of drinking the contents of a cup that caused Him inhuman anguish, mental agony, and made Him cringe away, almost repulsed by the thought of drinking it.

The physical fourth cup remained on the table in Jerusalem, but the reality that lay in its contents had taken hold of Him. He returned to the disciples, only to find them sleeping. He returned to His Father, presenting His trembling humanity, asking if there was another way to achieve Their goal. This is not a man afraid of facing death—it was the wine of the fourth cup! The wine in the third cup which He had designated as His blood shed for us, signified forgiveness and freedom from sin. In resurrection with Christ, it would bring us to the Father. But in the fourth cup, He saw the unspeakable suffering that He must endure in that blood shedding—the immense cost involved.

> There comes the moment when, with the totality of His being, He accepts the cost of 'My blood shed for you,' and He returns to the disciples, now fully the Man in charge of the events of this night.

He gave Himself to the arresting mob that came through the trees, led by Judas, and the night unfolded with every kind of dehumanizing suffering. His blood was shed throughout the night, but especially in His scourging. In these hours, He becomes our sin—our sin laid upon Him by Yahweh through the hands of wicked men. He willingly takes the iniquity of us all. He came under the sin of the world and carried it in His mortal body. He does not do something external to Him but internally becomes us. He is crucified, a death reserved for worthless criminals; and so hangs the Son of God, one with us in the Lie, the Darkness, and the sin of the world.

After a great darkness had shrouded the world, which mirrored what had taken place in Him, He cried out, "I thirst." He has been through unspeakable torture that has dehydrated Him almost to death, and He is about to die. At that moment, minutes from death, He cries out that He thirsts! A soldier hears Him and has compassion, not bringing Him water but wine on a sponge that He can suck into His mouth. He drinks and then cries "It is finished," the wine apparently signaling the finish. What was finished? Why could He not die without the sponge filled with wine? I believe this was the fourth cup of Passover, the cup He had repulsed in the Garden, the cup left on the table because the disciples could not drink this one. This cup He must drink to the last dregs in utter loneliness, embraced only by His Father who never left Him, and the Spirit who upheld Him. His faith in His Father's Presence never wavered.

> It was the Trinity event of love, limitless faith—the One in the Other finalized in His intentionally releasing Himself to death after having said to the Father, "Into Your hands I commit my spirit."

He extended the Passover meal to that sponge of wine. That was the fourth cup that Jesus drank, and so every detail that has happened since the third cup is historically part of the Meal of the New Covenant and expounds how it is the Blood of the New Covenant that brings us to participate in His life, free forever from the clutches of death.

In the chapters that follow, we will repeat these events, but in greater detail. This chapter is meant as a guide through the events of that night, as a compass that will bring you to the meaning of the Eucharist.

11. Who Is In Control?

As we move forward from the pivotal moments of the Last Supper, we turn our attention to the significant implications of the Eucharist. **This meal is not just a remembrance of His sacrifice; it is an invitation to participate in the very life of Christ.** Jesus is not only bringing about release from sin but bringing mankind out of the terrifying embrace of death into life that can never be interrupted by death or slowed by death—life that explodes into yet further life! This transformation is not just historical; it resonates deeply within us, assuring us that we too can live beyond the shadow of death. In the Eucharist, we partake of His flesh, boldly declaring, "It is finished!"

The Father gave the Son to bring to pass a predetermined will to exalt mankind to sit resting in perfect union with the Father through Christ, a will that the Son was in perfect harmony with, and that His human will must now be brought to say the final

"Yes!"—bringing the obedience of the human to cancel the disobedience of Adam.

The Son of God must get inside of death and *destroy it from the inside*. But He must *do this as man*, as the last Adam, and in it all, *listen only to the Father and reverse the choice of Adam, and reversing death*. This upturned the cosmos! The lie would be exposed. Mankind would see that he was taken captive by the Liar, and while man was enslaved, his inheritance was stolen. Jesus enters into that captivity, sets us free, and restores all that is rightfully ours.

Jesus showed stress as they came into the Garden:

> "And He took with Him Peter and James and John, and began to be very distressed and troubled. And He said to them, "My soul is deeply grieved to the point of death; remain here and keep watch." And He went a little beyond *them*, and fell to the ground and *began* to pray that if it were possible, the hour might pass Him by. And He was saying, "Abba! Father! All things are possible for You; remove this cup from Me; yet not what I will, but what You will." Mark 14:33-36

All the words used to describe His mental and emotional state that Mark writes describe pain, fear, loathing—taken to the ultimate limit—to the point He said they cause Him an anguish that brought Him right there to the point of death. To see Jesus in such agony, we must be careful that we do not think of Him as a man who is terrified of suffering and death. This is a horror, a terror that no man had or ever would face. He is looking into the cup, the fourth cup, that is the cup of Death—not merely dying at the end of physical life, but Death that is un-life, un-health, and that not merely passive but active, rising to meet Him and to destroy before He can actively use that death to stop Death in its path.

He was meeting the darkness that had held mankind since the great Lie took hold of the human in the Garden of Eden. Now, in this Garden, the Darkness rises up to destroy the light. John spoke of this in John 1.

> "In Him was life, and life was the Light of men. The Light shines in the darkness, and the darkness did not comprehend it." John 1:4-5

The word 'comprehend' portrays darkness as having personality and actively seeking to lay hold of the Light. It has the double meaning of aggressively seeking to lay hold of the light, to apprehend, to grasp it, all of which can be positive and describe darkness as seeking to find and submit to light. But it also has a negative meaning—to arrest, grasp hold, and throw it down with a view to destroying or rendering the light ineffective. It is this negative meaning that is used here in John 1. Jesus met the entity which is darkness and faced all it could do to destroy Him, but it failed.

The original purpose of creation—bringing forth the human to be in, abide in, participate in the life of God, as the image of God in the earth—is now to be restored. This is the subject of John 6 and the conversation that has been pursued to explain the Eucharist in John 14-16. This restoration cannot happen unless Man, the Last Adam, comes inside of Death and Darkness and destroys them by the power of Life, Light and Truth. He stood as a true Man to achieve this.

The words used in Matthew, Mark, and Luke to describe His mental and emotional condition in these moments before praying all speak of extreme sorrow, fear, agony, and anguish. Hebrews 2:15 describes mankind as living all their lives in the fear of death. Jesus is now experiencing, and speaking to Himself about, the terrors of death as known by mankind.

This went on for some time, and He returned to awaken the sleeping disciples. This fourth cup contained the agony, grief, and sorrow, pain of Jesus' entire being, a path He would tread alone. The disciples had asked to go with Him, but He had said, "*Where I am going, you cannot come*" John 8:21. It is the Abrahamic covenant, where although the covenant is made in Abraham's name, he cannot participate in its making, but could only watch while God—and God-as-Abraham—made the covenant.

It concluded with Jesus saying, "Not My will but Yours be done" Luke 22:42. This does not mean that He was crushed or His ego broken—that is never God's way. It means that His human will is brought into perfect sync with the Father, just as He, the eternal Son, had always been. Now, He is the Man who wills and acts in perfect harmony with the Father.

He then came and tells His disciples to "Get up and let us be going," just as the soldiers, led by the eager betrayer Judas, entered the Garden with torches held high. It began with betrayal—*the first sip of the agonies of the fourth cup!*

It was over. God the Son, in His humanity brought Himself fully in line with the Plan settled before time, before creation. Together with the Father and Spirit, He *had said the Amen to it*—there had been no dissenting voice. The Trinity agreed that the events of this night were the only way! He had become human without ceasing to be God, immersing Himself in the darkness, the sin of humanity, making it His own—*this was the only way!*

And God the Son, in His humanity, said the final "Yes!" there in the shadows of Gethsemane, not with a bent and trembling body, but standing erect, and with His human voice of authority, one with the Voice of the Three, *"Not My will but Yours be done!"* He would endure the sufferings of this night, and enter death as every man, woman, and child, loving us to the end. When He would rise from the dead, He would have brought about release from all sin for all humans, carrying everyone to be carried into and through death to resurrection and life in joyous union with the Three in One. As He had said a few hours earlier, *"I am the way, and the truth, and the life, no one comes to the Father but through Me"* (John 14:6). And the way—the only way—was for Christ to carry the entire race of humans through death to resurrection.

He stands in front of the mob: the Roman battalion, the Temple police, a kind of private army to guard all things Jewish. From the man crying in agony of soul half an hour ago to this man standing with the authority of a decision made and a commitment surrendered to, He stands in the path of the advancing soldiers carrying torches lighting the way through the dark garden. Others carried swaying lanterns to light the immediate path in front of them. The swinging swords at the belts of the Romans mirrored the torches, as did their breastplates. The Temple priests and some members of the Sanhedrin formed a tight group at the front, intent on seeing and hearing all that would happen that night. Judas led the way, trying to put on a bold front but showing fear of what would happen in the next few minutes.

Jesus addresses them, "Who are you seeking?" His voice is loud and commanding enough to stop them in their tracks. The Roman commander steps forward, saying, "Jesus the Nazarene," and by that time Judas has reached Him and kisses Him on the cheek. Jesus looks with deep pain into the furtive eyes of this frightened man, "Do you betray the Son of Man *with a kiss?*" Turning His attention to the commander, Jesus responds, "I AM!" It is the name of Yahweh given to Moses at the burning bush: I AM THAT I AM. Jesus had used it sparingly in the last three years, but never releasing its power in this fashion. Tonight, it physically hit the mob—an enormous energy force that laid them on their backs! They are disarmed—their swords, shields, clubs, and sticks go flying into the air—as Judas' great plans to betray crumble, and the priests, Pharisees, Temple guards, and Roman soldiers all lie foolishly on their backs, helpless beside each other, like so many roaches kicking their legs trying to gain some traction.

Some manage to kneel but now hesitate, looking terrified at Jesus, reluctant to be the first on their feet! They lie wondering what just happened—what will He do next? Is He a Jewish magician?!

He has rendered them helpless with two words. But there was no anger or pent-up rage in His voice; He is not ordering them to leave! Yet He is a terrifying sight, towering above them, exuding absolute authority over all lying and kicking in front of Him. At the same time, a faint smile dances around the edge of His mouth, visible through the blood they now notice on His face and neck, shed in the last agonizing hour of prayer.

One man screams, his face covered in blood, holding his ear in his hand. Peter stands awkwardly by, wondering what to do next —a fisherman who had just used his sword like a fishing pole, swinging down on the servant of the High Priest, managing to miss his head and only sever his ear. Jesus walks over, bends down and puts the ear back where it belongs, immediately healing it. As He stands up, He orders Peter to put away his sword; this is not a night for fighting their enemies.

> One thing is certain to the men now beginning to get back on their feet: this Man is in control of everything happening tonight.

They had been sent to bring Him to the residence of the High Priest, remembering their commander telling them, "Don't worry, He's simple, harmless. Don't know why they sent this many soldiers. He's a carpenter from up in Galilee, wouldn't kill a fly. He's a healer and weeps over people hurting! Puts His arms around the sick and heals them." He's harmless, they told us. Said we would be home by one o'clock this morning at the latest! I don't know if we'll be home at all tonight!

Jesus speaks again, "Who are you seeking?" His voice is soft and gentle. The commander manages to get the words out, his throat constricted by fear, that they are seeking Jesus of Nazareth—he tenses waiting for another surge of energy, maybe setting him in a tree top! But nothing happens. Jesus identifies Himself and offers Himself to be arrested and tried. He submits to the soldiers; the time has come when He is to suffer at the hands of wicked men, and it involves pain, unspeakable anguish of body, but also the depths of mental and emotional pain, rejection, forsakenness, and loneliness.

> *Before He hands Himself over to the hands of His torturers, He makes it plain who oversees the events of this night.*

Jesus has quietly established who is in control. The point is made, and soldiers and priests would tell the story to their children and their families at every Passover. Jesus is the overseer of all that priest and Roman authorities might do; His words do more than all the swords in Gethsemane that night could do. This also underscores for all future generations that He was not taken by surprise or by human strategy. He had established that this is not an ambush; not a betrayal by Judas in the sense that they had captured Him at His most vulnerable.

Has Judas betrayed Him? Judas has the sickening feeling that he didn't betray Jesus when he led the soldiers and priests to His private clearing in the Garden—Jesus was ready for them, and Judas' kiss was unnecessary! This is not an unexpected military move to capture Him against His will. *It's a trap that the soldiers and leaders of the people have walked into!* He is not arrested by soldiers before He arrests them! And all the wicked plans they have for this night of torture and terror must pass His inspection! *They could not hurt this man except with His permission,* by the intention of God to shed His blood—the blood of God—and bring Him to the point where He yields up His spirit. They did not kill Him, He chose to die.

In the chaos, Jesus' disciples begin to disappear into the Garden, afraid they would be the next arrested. He treads the next hours alone, just as He had said earlier, "Where I am going, you cannot come!"

Hesitantly, the soldiers come to put ropes around Him, leading Him as a helpless lamb to the slaughter. Everyone knows He could speak just two words—His Name—and bring the entire operation to a halt! Whatever He endures that night, He has established that He actively allows it with intention.

The religious leaders, the masterminds behind the plan, are the first to pour out their hatred upon Him, followed by the Roman governor's soldiers, brutally beating and scourging Him, before sending Him to be crucified.

> "Then they (the religious leaders) spat in His face and beat Him with their fists; and others slapped Him, and said, "Prophesy to us, You Christ; who is the one who hit You?" Matthew 26:67-68

> "Then the soldiers of the governor took Jesus into the Praetorium and gathered the whole Roman cohort around Him. They stripped Him and put a scarlet

> robe on Him. And after twisting together a crown of thorns, they put it on His head, and a reed in His right hand; and they knelt before Him and mocked Him, saying, "Hail, King of the Jews!" They spat on Him and took the reed and began to beat Him on the head. After they had mocked Him, they took the scarlet robe off Him and put His own garments back on Him and led Him away to crucify Him." Matthew 27:27-31

> "I gave My back to those who strike Me, and My cheeks to those who pluck out the beard; I did not cover My face from humiliation and spitting." Isaiah 50:6

The Roman torture as a prelude to the crucifixion was whipping. A leather whip with thongs tipped at each end with pieces of bone, iron, and jagged stone, was in the hands of a sadist who could place the deadly lashes where he wanted with the precision of a surgeon, bringing a man to the brink of death. The lashes bit deeply into His skin and fascia, tearing through the skin and cutting into the muscle, exposing His ribs and organs. The whip wrapped around His body, gripping His stomach in a deadly embrace.

The prophet shuddered as he wrote Isaiah 53; this Man he described did not even look like a man, and all who saw Him, looked in horror.

> "He was despised and forsaken of men, a man of sorrows and acquainted with grief; and like one from whom men hide their face He was despised, and we did not esteem Him." Isaiah 53:3

And as the prophet also described this Man in Isaiah 52:14:

> "[For many the Servant of God became an object of horror; many were astonished at Him.] His face and His whole appearance were marred more than any man's, and His form beyond that of the sons of men — but just as many were astonished at Him…" (AMP)
>
> "Just as many were astonished at you, My people, so His appearance was marred more than any man and His form more than the sons of men." (NASB)
>
> "But many were amazed when they saw him. His face was so disfigured He seemed hardly human, and from his appearance, one would scarcely know he was a man." (NLT)
>
> "But he didn't begin that way. At first everyone was appalled. He didn't even look human — a ruined face, disfigured past recognition." (MSG)

And His torture and suffering continued:

> "Pilate then took Jesus and scourged Him. And the soldiers twisted together a crown of thorns and put it on His head

and put a purple robe on Him; and they began to come up to Him and say, "Hail, King of the Jews!" and to give Him slaps in the face." John 19:1-3

"They shouted back, "Crucify Him!" But Pilate said to them, "Why, what evil has He done?" But they shouted all the more, "Crucify Him!" Wishing to satisfy the crowd, Pilate released Barabbas for them, and after having Jesus scourged, he handed Him over to be crucified. The soldiers took Him away into the palace (that is, the Praetorium), and they called together the whole Roman cohort. They dressed Him up in purple, and after twisting a crown of thorns, they put it on Him; and they began to acclaim Him, "Hail, King of the Jews!" They kept beating His head with a reed, and spitting on Him, and kneeling and bowing before Him. After they had mocked Him, they took the purple robe off Him and put His own garments on Him. And they led Him out to crucify Him." Mark 15:13-20

"Those passing by were hurling abuse at Him, wagging their heads, and saying, "Ha! You who are going to destroy the temple and rebuild it in three days, save Yourself, and come down from the cross!" In the same way the chief

> priests also, along with the scribes,
> were mocking Him among themselves
> and saying, "He saved others; He
> cannot save Himself. Let this Christ,
> the King of Israel, now come down
> from the cross, so that we may see and
> believe!" Those who were crucified
> with Him were also insulting Him."
> Mark 15:29-32

But in between being pushed through the streets of Jerusalem, in the dark of night, He was mocked, spat on, His beard torn from His face, tearing the flesh with it. A crown made from branches covered with long thorns like spikes was jammed into His skull, boring jagged holes in His scalp, causing blood to flow profusely, matting His hair, and running down His face into His beard, already bloody from sweating blood as He had prayed in Gethsemane.

12. The Day Death Died

Pilate brought Him out—how could He stand after 40 lashes had mauled His body? Pilate sneered as he pushed Jesus forward, saying, "Behold the Man!" John 19:5.

Why would we want to stay for a moment to contemplate such savagery? Because it was all inflicted—from spittle mingling with the blood on His face to the leather whip with its bloody thongs—on the body of the incarnate God! This is the body that God assumed when He became human! This is God in the act of giving His body to us!

Why? It is 100% for us—there is no reason He would be here but for us. Translations vary: "My body given for you," "My body for you," "My body broken for you." Note the phrase that never changes, 'for you.' He has thrown Himself into the horrific pain, hatred, and rage of this world in its darkness and made it His own for each one, for every human being—for you!

"Behold the Man!" sneered Pilate at the mangled man whose robe was scarlet with the blood that seeped through. Look at the One who is your king!

The Temple, the religious—not caring about the condition of the man they saw—screamed even more, drunk with hatred, "Crucify Him!"—the words to a Jew meant "Damn Him to hell!"

Beyond words to describe, beyond all definition of pain, the soldiers placed the rough wood of the upright of the cross on His ravaged back. Then, pushing Him with spears, they forced Him to the road that led to Golgotha, the place of execution. We have a word in English, *excruciating*, which is an imported Latin word that means *'out of the cross'*—meaning a pain akin to the pain of Jesus on the cross. But the word makes a mockery of pain!

Crucifixion was invented as the ultimate torture machine. It was not to be likened to the death sentence of other nations—hanging, electrocution, gas chambers, shooting—all of which aim at immediate death. But crucifixion brought the victim to the edge of death and left them hanging on a crossbar for days or even weeks. Crucifixion was not invented to kill a person but to torture them beyond the limits of human thought. It produced unspeakable pain as the victims would have to hoist themselves up on the nail through their feet to take a gasp of air; for one breath the entire body was wracked with pain. The body, hanging by nails through the wrists, constricted the lungs, and if left hanging, the victim would suffocate.

A helpless, naked body nailed to a torture machine, their nakedness mocked and laughed at by the mob, added sexual abuse to the mental agony. They were helpless before the birds that would perch on them to peck their faces. Screaming thirst, burning sun—all added to the torture. When there was the necessity of a swift death, the soldiers went from body to body and broke their legs so they could no longer push up to breathe. Such necessity existed that weekend, for it was Passover, and the Jews, having accomplished the crucifixion of the One they hated, now demanded that the show be over by the time their religious services began that evening!

Much of that blood shedding was in the scourging that tore the skin and muscles from His back and sides, and in the pulling off of His cheeks when they tore His beard from His face.

The wounds that made Him look like something other than human were made by sin—sin in thought, feeling, word, and action left the physical mark of sin, a 'real estate presence in the body.' The scourging brings healing to the multidimensions of sickness—of spirit, mind, emotion, and body—that cut into His body, leaving their mark, their unique shape in the body. In this way, He bore sin and sickness in His body.

It was three in the afternoon when darkness descended not only here but recorded elsewhere on the planet.

In the eerie darkness, Jesus spoke loud enough for all to hear, "My God, My God, why have You forsaken Me?" That was when the Man who is God fully entered the utter loneliness of mankind, believing themselves to be separated from a disinterested deity who has abandoned them to their darkness.

This must not be thought of as God the Father turning His back on the Son because He, the Father, is too holy to look at Him bearing the sin of the world. That is too foolish to consider—that God the Father is more holy than Jesus! Too foolish to say that God the Son can be made one with our sin and say, "Father, forgive them; they know not what they do!" but God the Father cannot look at mankind in sin. When His Son, in the act of limitless love, has taken sin and made it His own, the Father cannot look at His own Son? That would mean God is divided and the Trinity has fallen apart!

Such an idea would portray a god who is the monster of our worst fears—one who has forsaken us and left us to our sin. Jesus would then be the One whose mission was to change the Father's mind about us! Jesus would be saving us from God! Such a Father is a creature of religion's deceived and darkened imagination and could never be described as Love, for 1 Corinthians 13:5 assures us, "Love does not keep a record of wrongs!"

Most Jewish people of those days memorized the Psalms while teenagers! In a conversation, if a certain psalm contributed to the subject as they talked casually, someone would quote the first verse of the psalm they believed would move the conversation along. Everyone knew the entire psalm and hearing the first verse was all they needed to have the entire psalm repeating in their head. As the darkness descended, Jesus on the cross quotes the first verse of Psalm 22. The first verses give the most vivid portrayal of what was taking place. But then verses 22 and those that follow assure the reader that *although that is what it looked like, it was by no means the truth.* Rather, the Father is the source of His hope and strength to carry this through!

> "I will tell of Your name to my brethren; in the midst of the assembly, I will praise You. You who fear the Lord, praise Him; all you descendants of Jacob, glorify Him, and stand in awe of Him, all you descendants of Israel. *For He has not despised nor abhorred the affliction of the afflicted; nor has He hidden His face from him; but when he cried to Him for help, He heard.*" Psalm 22:22-24

Amazingly, He did not raise His voice against His torturers. This is of such importance that it was spoken of in a 500-year-old prophecy and Peter's report of the event.

> "He was oppressed, and He was afflicted, yet He did not open His mouth; like a lamb that is led to slaughter, and like a sheep that is silent before its shearers, so He did not open His mouth." Isaiah 53:7

Pilate, utterly frustrated, demands Jesus speak to him.

> "... who committed no sin, nor was any deceit found in His mouth; and while being reviled, He did not revile in return; while suffering, He uttered no

threats, but kept entrusting Himself to Him who judges righteously; and He Himself bore our sins in His body on the cross, so that we might die to sin and live to righteousness; for by His wounds you were healed." 1 Peter 2:22-24

The only words He spoke were, "Father, forgive them; for they do not know what they are doing!" Luke 23:34

When someone hurls insults and curses at us, it is natural to deny their lies, to push back with words or force if possible—we are saying as clearly as we can that their words and actions do not fit us. This One had made it plain what He could do to defend Himself; His silence was even more a mystery. Why does He not push back with the force He had shown in the Garden? Of all people, this One is innocent, blameless, being treated as the lowest criminal! We would expect Him to push back and deny what they say. We want Him to finish what He began at the Garden and let them know who He is—lay them flat on their backs. But He, by His silence, accepts their words and actions as if they were true and belonged to Him.

And that is what He was doing! He forged a relationship with mankind at our very worst; when sin has come to full maturity and spat its venom on Jesus, He embraces what they—what we—said and did, and in effect says, "Give it to Me!"

It is a fact that all our thoughts and feelings are not floating clouds that just disappear over some cosmic horizon and are no more. They are solid, taking up space, or, as Dr. Caroline Leaf says, 'thoughts are real, physical things that occupy mental real estate.'* Each organ in our body has storage space for certain thoughts and feelings—for real guilt and shame, for traumatic events, moments of anguish and terror.

With every act of hatred and mockery contained in the spittle, with every punch from the soldiers, and every lash of the whip, the sin of the world and its grief and sorrow was literally laid on Jesus. He chose to take it and bear it in His body, and in doing so, ravaged His body until He no longer looked like a human being. The sin of every man focused on the body of Jesus Christ and left its scar.

> "He was despised and forsaken of men, a man of sorrows and acquainted with grief; and like one from whom men hide their face He was despised, and we did not esteem Him. Surely our griefs He Himself bore, and our sorrows He carried; yet we ourselves esteemed Him stricken, smitten of God, and afflicted. But He was pierced through for our transgressions, He was crushed for our iniquities; the chastening for our well-being fell upon Him, and by His scourging we are healed. All of us like sheep have gone

---

* Caroline Leaf, *Switch On Your Brain: The Key to Peak Happiness, Thinking, and Health* (Nashville, TN: Thomas Nelson, 2013), 24.

> astray, each of us has turned to his
> own way; but the Lord has caused the
> iniquity of us all to fall on Him."
> Isaiah 53:3-6

Note the words 'grief and sorrow.' Combined, they describe the greatest pain, the anguish of body and mind, emotional pain, involving depression, hopeless despair. But also, these are Hebrew words for sickness and disease and are translated as such in Matthew 8:17.

Jesus taking our sin, for many people, is a vague idea, but these words in Isaiah 53 describe something very tangible tearing at His body and the pain of mind and emotion.

Celebrating the Eucharist, we eat His body with speechless wonder that our sin, grief, sorrow, guilt, shame, fear, despair, and hopelessness—all was taken into the human body of God in the ravaging of the human body of Jesus at a time on the clock and a date of the month. *If it is all upon Him to the point that He became sin for every human person, became our curse, then it cannot be upon us at the same time.*

> "... and while being reviled, He did not
> revile in return; while suffering, He
> uttered no threats, but kept entrusting
> Himself to Him who judges right-
> eously; and He Himself bore our sins
> in His body on the cross, so that we
> might die to sin and live to right-

eousness; for by His wounds, you were healed." 1 Peter 2:23-24

"In his person he bore our sins in his own body upon the tree and thus brought closure to every distorted pattern of sin's influence upon us; we were made alive unto righteousness; we were healed by the blows he took in his body." 1 Peter 2:24 (Mirror Bible)

"The next day he saw Jesus coming to him and said, "Behold, the Lamb of God who takes away the sin of the world!" John 1:29

"Behold the Lamb of God; this is the one who would lift the sin of the cosmos like an anchor from the sea floor, for mankind to sail free." (Cosmos = the entire human family and their social structures.) John 1:29 (Mirror Bible)

Sin is not what we do; rather, *sin* is being out of sync with your true identity and, so, missing out on your sonship and knowing the love of the Trinity.

In Christ, God lifted sin up and away! There was nothing left for religion to try to deal with. The extreme, extravagant, scandalous, shocking, and embarrassing love of God that demands nothing from us, only that we trust who He shows Himself to be, has been revealed.

This was brought about by the shedding of blood as the darkness attacked as did Satan and the other powers of darkness. This brings us to our own identity—all of this is what it cost Him to come where we are, to bring us the news of forgiveness, and take us in Himself to be where He is with the Father. Our infinite worth is spelled out in the fourth cup.

We are worth all that took place in the fourth cup!

He enters and experiences as His own the great darkness. He cried out of our deepest selves, where we live in the illusion of an angry god who has abandoned us and leaves us to rot forever. It was in the middle of this that the veil of the Temple—the separating curtain between man and God's visible presence—was ripped in two to declare no more separation! The darkness lifts and He is ready to bring everything to conclusion. He asks for a drink, "I thirst."

Consider the state of His body to be able to ask for anything! That He should wait for the end before asking, when all that had gone before dehydrated Him to the max. They bring him wine and vinegar on a sponge, with a hyssop branch being the carrier of the wine. Having drunk from the sponge, He cries, "It is finished!" I believe *that wine* was the fourth cup that was not drunk at the rooftop room table but carried to this moment, thus including all of the events of suffering and death into the *new* Passover meal. The kingdom of God has come through the shedding of His blood. Now—ready to plunge into death—He commits Himself to the Father and yields up His spirit. He dies.

We partake in the Eucharist to eat, drink, and participate in His flesh and blood. Yet we also

stand afar, worshiping the great love that placed such value on us, as He alone drank the fourth cup—finishing the work of our redemption.

He has finished all that can be done here. He has received, at the hands of wicked men, into His sinless body, the sin and grief of the world. He now will go, God in His humanity, carrying us at our worst with Him into His death. He bore or carried our sin—where did He carry that sin? Peter made it plain that it was *in His body* that the sin of the world was carried and taken into death.

> "Who committed no sin, nor was any deceit found in His mouth; and while being reviled, He did not revile in return; while suffering, He uttered no threats, but kept entrusting *Himself* to Him who judges righteously; and He Himself bore our sins in His body on the cross, so that we might die to sin and live to righteousness; for by His wounds you were healed." 1 Peter 2:22-24

> "And although you were formerly alienated and hostile in mind, engaged in evil deeds, yet He has *now reconciled you in His fleshly body through death*, in order to present you before Him holy and blameless and beyond reproach — if indeed you continue in the faith firmly established and steadfast, and not moved away from the hope of the gospel that you have heard, which was

> proclaimed in all creation under heaven." Colossians 1:21-23

> "In God's mind mankind is associated in Christ; in His blood sacrifice we were ransomed; our redemption was secured; our sins were completely done away with…He initiated the reconciliation of all things to Himself …He has now fully reconciled and restored you to your original design. *He accomplished this in dying our death in a human body*; *He fully represented us in order to fully present us again in blameless innocence, face to face with God; with no sense of guilt, suspicion, regret or accusation; all charges against us are officially canceled."* Colossians 1:14, 20, 21, 22 (Mirror Bible)

He deliberately submitted to death—our death. He has never been there before. No man has been there to return. The graves around the city spoke volumes that the grave was a portal no man ever returned from. Those who had been raised from the dead lived for a while but, like all humans, died in the end.

Jesus on the cross contemplates the death that He must go into, carrying all of us with Him. He will die *as us*, die our death; our sin will be gone, and forgiveness announced. His only guarantee of returning from death was the Father raising Him from the dead. As He stepped into death, He said, "Father, into Your hands I commit My spirit" Luke 23:46. He then, with intention, gave up His spirit, and He died, His lifeless body hanging on a cross. Neither the Jewish leaders nor the mighty Roman Empire killed Him—He gave Himself to us and to our death before they had a chance to kill Him.

> "No one has taken it away from Me, but I lay it down on My own initiative. I have authority to lay it down, and I have authority to take it up again."
> John 10:18

The soldiers came to break His legs and were amazed that He was dead already. One soldier took his spear and thrust it into Jesus' side, up into His heart, and John noted that a rush of blood and water came out. Blood with water tells us He died of a broken heart.

He was gone, carrying our sin in His ravaged body, scarred with the grief and sorrow sin had brought. He carried *in His mortal body* the sin of mankind. If He did not return from death, the hope of all peoples perished with Him; sin would have been too big for Him to carry, and death would have won.

The third day, He rises, having been healed of all the marks of His bearing sin except for the trophy marks of crucifixion. The real estate of sin and sickness was wiped out, cleansed from the body. His dead body not only came back to life, but He lived never to die again. Death had been defeated; death died, and Jesus lived and lived!

> "Do not be afraid; I am the first and the last, and the living One; and I was

> dead, and behold, I am alive forevermore, and I have the keys of death and of Hades." Revelation 1:17-18

He appeared to Mary, to those traveling home to Emmaus, and then to the gathered disciples in a room in Jerusalem. His prime concern was that they knew that He, in the fullness of His humanity, was alive. Telling them plainly He was not a ghost, a bodiless spirit, He offered them His body for the gathered disciples to touch, and He showed them a perfect body except for the wounds in hands, feet, and side. He then asked if they had something to eat, and He sat at a table and ate it in front of them.

What did it mean? The torn and ravaged body of Jesus that was laid in the tomb now stood healed of all wounds, leaving only the evidence that He had been crucified, but now stood alive—the Living One, Source of life that now knew no death.

The psalmist describes the passing of one who has bullied and controlled but now is gone: "Then he passed away, and lo, he was no more; I sought for him, but he could not be found" Psalm 37:36.

You, along with every person to the end of time, were there, included in His all-inclusive death. That *you* under the control of sin and death is gone; that *you* are no more. You can look for that *you,* but that *you* cannot be found any more than you can find the suffering, crucified Jesus! *You* not only died with Him, *you* were raised from the dead in Him and *you* ascended to be seated with Him in the heavenly realm.

Remember that He went through the horror of the cross for every person. His body, healed, and cleansed of all wounds—internal and external—meant that the sin He carried in His body was no more. *Therefore we, each one of us—humans, everyone and everywhere—were as free from sin as the radiant Man standing in front of us.*

> "So what do we do? Keep on sinning so God can keep on forgiving? I should hope not! If we've left the country where sin is sovereign, how can we still live in our old house there? Or didn't you realize we packed up and left there for good? That is what happened in baptism. When we went under the water, we left the old country of sin behind; when we came up out of the water, we entered into the new country of grace — a new life in a new land!"
> Romans 6:1-3(MSG)

That's what baptism into the life of Jesus means. When we are lowered into the water, it is like the burial of Jesus; when we are raised up out of the water, it is like the resurrection of Jesus. Each of us is raised into a light-filled world by our Father so that we can see where we're going in our new grace-sovereign country. Could it be any clearer? *Our old way of life was nailed to the Cross with Christ, a decisive end to that sin-miserable life* — no longer at sin's every beck and call! What we believe is this: If we get included in Christ's sin-conquering death, we also get included in His life-saving resurrection. We know that when Jesus was raised from the dead it was a signal of the end of death-as-the-end. Never again will death have the last word. When Jesus died, He took sin down with Him, but alive He brings God down to us. From now on, think of it this way: Sin speaks a dead language that means nothing to you; God speaks your mother tongue, and you hang on every word. You are dead to sin and alive to God. That's what Jesus did.

> "That means you must not give sin a vote in the way you conduct your lives. Don't give it the time of day. Don't even run little errands that are connected with that old way of life. Throw yourselves wholeheartedly and full-time — remember, you've been raised from the dead! — into God's way of doing things. Sin can't tell you how to live. After all, you're not living under that old tyranny any longer. You're living in the freedom of God."
> Romans 6:1-14 (MSG)

> "But God, being rich in mercy, because of His great love with which He loved us, even when we were dead in our transgressions, *made us alive together with Christ* (by grace you have been saved), and *raised us up with Him, and seated us with Him in the heavenly places in Christ Jesus*, so that in the ages to come He might show the surpassing riches of His grace in kindness toward us in Christ Jesus. For by grace you have been saved through faith; and that not of yourselves, it is the gift of God; not as a result of works, so that no one may boast. For we are His workmanship,

created in Christ Jesus for good works, which God prepared beforehand so that we would walk in them." Ephesians 2:4-10

"You yourselves are a case study of what he does. At one time you all had your backs turned to God, thinking rebellious thoughts of him, giving him trouble every chance you got. 22 But now, by giving himself completely at the Cross, actually dying for you, Christ brought you over to God's side and put your lives together, whole and holy in his presence. 23 You don't walk away from a gift like that! You stay grounded and steady in that bond of trust, constantly tuned in to the Message, careful not to be distracted or diverted. There is no other Message — just this one. Every creature under heaven gets this same Message. I, Paul, am a messenger of this Message." Colossians 1:21-23 (MSG)

"God rescued us from dead-end alleys and dark dungeons. He's set us up in the kingdom of the Son he loves so much, the Son who got us out of the pit we were in, got rid of the sins we were doomed to keep repeating." Colossians 1:13-14 (MSG)

He now says, "This is My body given to you…" We eat, not *to get* this breathtaking reality, but *because we have been awakened to see that we were and are in Him, and now celebrate this reality!* It is now so! We can only receive what is ours, knowing we could not and cannot pay for this salvation. It is secured and announced by the Lord Jesus Christ Himself. He is our salvation. He stood *as us*, and now we stand in Him; as He does, we celebrate, rejoicing with Him.

13. Meal of Healing and Health

I have found that many who subscribe to the belief in Christ dwelling within us become upset—sometimes even angry—when we discuss the idea of eating and drinking of His ascended flesh and blood. This practice graphically declares that He is the risen Person within us.

Has the church become afraid of the mystery of the miraculous? Is that why so many would rather attribute miracles of healing to the devil than give glory to God? Is it because they have determined that God is holy—and, in their view, holy means rage at sin and sinners, with judgment coming in the form of sickness and death—so any healing must be working against the will of the god-monster they've created?

Jesus did not merely do something *for* us, exterior both to Him and us. He is the gift. He is all that He accomplished for all was accomplished *in* Him. His sufferings were physical, mental, and emotional and He bore not only our spiritual sickness—our sins—but also our physical, mental, and emotional sickness, and all that falls under the category of *dis*-ease.

He died, His mortal body bearing the physical marks of bearing our sin and sickness, the pain of mental and emotional disease, to the point where He no longer resembled a human being!

In resurrection His body was restored—no longer mortal—but as one beyond the touch of death, with all evidence of sin, human sorrow, and sickness removed. This transition from death to life is the *mystery* we celebrate in the Eucharist

In His ascension to glory with the Father, He chose to retain only the wounds that He carries as trophies—the nail prints in hands and feet and the spear gash in His side.

We were, and are in Him. He suffered and died *as* us. When He rose, we rose with Him, in Him, and there is no physical evidence of our sin or disease—His body is alive in resurrection life.

> "Or do you not know that all of us who have been baptized into Christ Jesus have been baptized into His death? Therefore we have been buried with Him through baptism into death, so that as Christ was raised from the dead through the glory of the Father, so we too might walk in newness of life. For if we have become united with Him in

the likeness of His death, certainly we shall also be in the likeness of His resurrection, knowing this, that our old self was crucified with Him, in order that our body of sin might be done away with, so that we would no longer be slaves to sin; for he who has died is freed from sin.

Now if we have died with Christ, we believe that we shall also live with Him, knowing that Christ, having been raised from the dead, is never to die again; death no longer is master over Him. For the death that He died, He died to sin once for all; but the life that He lives, He lives to God. Even so consider yourselves to be dead to sin, but alive to God in Christ Jesus." Romans 6:3-11

"But God, being rich in mercy, because of His great love with which He loved us, even when we were dead in our transgressions, made us alive together with Christ (by grace you have been saved), and raised us up with Him, and seated us with Him in the heavenly places in Christ Jesus, so that in the ages to come He might show the surpassing riches of His grace in kindness toward us in Christ Jesus. For by grace you have been saved through faith; and that not of yourselves, it is the gift of

God; not as a result of works, so that no one may boast. For we are His workmanship, created in Christ Jesus for good works, which God prepared beforehand so that we would walk in them." Ephesians 2:4-10

In the languages of the Bible, there is no clear distinction between the physical and the spiritual. The Greek word for salvation is *sozo*, but the word for physical healing is also *sozo*! This duality highlights that in Christ, our salvation encompasses every facet of our existence—spiritual, physical, and emotional.

In the Gospels, we read both, "Your faith has *saved* you" and "Your faith has *healed* you." It was the translator's choice to make a distinction between *saved* and *healed*, but there is none in the original language. Have you ever wondered why Jesus said to the Pharisees, "Which is easier to say, 'Your sins are forgiven you', or to say, 'Take up your bed and walk'?" Much of the church finds it easy to assure people of forgiveness, but would find it impossible to speak the words of physical healing! Yet, as Jesus plainly stated, there is no difference.

There is no separate word for spiritual salvation and another for physical, mental, or emotional sickness. In Christ, the human is saved from sickness and disease in the totality of their being. All that He assumed and made His own, He saved. In taking on our bodies, minds, and emotions, He heals us in our entirety. To save us, He became our sin, sickness, and death, saving us from the inside. In His resurrection, through the Spirit, He gives Himself as the Healer—healed and healing. He restores the human body from whatever state sin has brought it to.

Saved from sin is not just a rescue operation from bad behavior! It is the healing of the sinful person in their total humanity—their body, mind, emotions, and their relationship with the Father. I am not saying that sickness is because we have sinned, but I am saying that sin is not something caged in our spirit. It leaves its trail of futility and darkness in our mind and emotions. It is in our darkened mind, emotions, and imagination that the pathways of sin are conceived and fully formed before being passed on to our choices and behaviors.

Sin should not be limited to what we have done to provoke God's anger against us, a limiting misconception rooted in the false belief that God is a deity of wrath, eager to punish us. But God is love, and because of that, there is a vast area of life we have not lived, which has caused pain in the heart of the Father. Love opens its heart with the possibility of being hurt, and God can be hurt by our blindness to being His sons and daughters—by our reluctance to cry out, "Abba Father." The years we were not bringing forth His love in kindness, gentleness, forgiveness and compassion. The pain the father feels is not as much from the younger son's life in the far country, but from the fake self-righteousness of the older son.

> Jesus gave His mortal body, shedding His life blood, to bring us out of the darkness of death, saving us into the light of His love in the totality of our being.

The greatest chapter in the Old Testament, Isaiah 53, presents us with salvation covering the entirety of our human existence. This has been hidden in the limitation of translation.

> "Surely our griefs He Himself bore, and our sorrows He carried. Yet we ourselves esteemed Him stricken, smitten of God and afflicted. But He was pierced through for our transgressions, He was crushed for our iniquities. The chastening for our well-being fell upon Him, and by His scourging we are healed. All of us like sheep have gone astray, each of us has turned to his own way. But the Lord has caused the iniquity of us all to fall on Him." Isaiah 53:4-6

> "He was despised and rejected and forsaken by men, a Man of *sorrows and pains, and acquainted with grief and sickness*; and like One from Whom men *hide their faces* He was *despised*, and we did *not appreciate His worth* or have *any esteem* for Him. Surely, He has borne our *griefs (sicknesses, weaknesses, and distresses)* and carried our *sorrows and pains [of punishment],* yet we [ignorantly] considered Him stricken, smitten, and afflicted by God [as if with leprosy]. But He was wounded for our transgressions, He was bruised for our guilt and iniquities; the chastisement [needful to obtain] peace and well-being for us was upon

> Him, and with the stripes [that wounded] Him we are healed and made whole." Isaiah 53:3-5 (AMP)

> "When evening came, they brought to Him many who were *demon-possessed; and He cast out the spirits with a word and healed all who were ill.* This was to fulfill what was spoken through Isaiah the prophet: "He Himself took our infirmities and carried away our diseases." Matthew 8:16-18

Placed together, the words, *grief* and *sorrow* describe every pain the human can experience. *Grief* refers to the specific pain of sickness, infirmity, and disease in the human body, mind, emotions, as well as the sickness of mankind's spirit—the darkness of the Lie that we are separated from God. *Sorrow* encompasses every other kind of pain: the pain of broken relationships that have fallen apart, failure in business, the collapse of society, and when cities and nations are sick with the lies of the darkness. It also describes the experience of being caught in the crossfire of other people's rage and failures in life. It is the dark shroud over a person's life, living in regret for past actions, or blinders of a poverty mindset, living under the rule of "I am not, I have not, I cannot."

> "When Jesus came into Peter's home, He saw his mother-in-law lying sick in bed with a fever. He touched her hand, and the fever left her; and she got up and waited on Him. When evening came, they brought to Him many who were demon-possessed; and He cast out the

> spirits with a word and healed all who were ill. This was to fulfill what was spoken through Isaiah the prophet: "He Himself took our *sicknesses and carried away our diseases.*" Matthew 8:14-17

> "He Himself took our *incapacities (weaknesses; infirmities; sicknesses)* and then lifted up and bore *the diseases* aloft." Matthew 8:17 (Jonathan Mitchell New Testament)

> "And thus He fulfilled what was spoken by the prophet Isaiah, He Himself *took [in order to carry away] our weaknesses and infirmities and bore away our diseases*." Matthew 8:17 (AMP)

When He cried, "It is finished," total healing and wholeness were included—not just in a spiritual dimension, but for the whole person. Healing and restoration are for the entirety of our being.

The expression *savior* and *saved* were used everyday language during the time of the New Testament, and they were very physical. These words were used to describe a doctor of medicine and the cure of physical ailments. Not only medical doctors but also first responders were designated as *saviors* because they *saved* people from mortal danger, all disease, and demonic oppression.

In the Eucharist, we are presented with the Blood of Christ, with the words, "This is the Blood of Christ, the cup of your salvation"—we could very correctly say, "the Blood of Christ, the cup of your healing." I have seen on multiple occasions the real presence of the Savior and Healer making people whole as they receive the body and blood of Christ. Very early in my journey, I was invited to share the Eucharist with a group of nuns—how that happened or where it was, I have since forgotten. I didn't know that 50 years later I would write a book, and it would be helpful to have the facts of names and places!

As the nuns came to receive the body and the blood of Christ, I heard a loud cry directed to God. I did not know at the time was that one of the nuns was blind, and after she received the Eucharist, she returned to her seat healed!

Many have testified to being given "peace that passes human comprehension" as they have received and experienced salvation from anxiety and fears—a great healing of mind and emotions.

The Hebrew word translated as 'peace' in Hebrew is *shalom*, an all-encompassing word that speaks of an entire life in peace and giving peace. *It means, peace, prosperity, wholeness, success, and well-being.* Jesus took upon Himself everything that was the absence or opposite of peace, experiencing it in His own body, wracking His mind and tearing His emotions. Then, having become one with it, took it to death in Himself. In His resurrection we are united to Him—the peace of God that passes human comprehension.

> "The chastening for our well-being fell

upon Him, and by His scourging we are healed." Isaiah 53:5

"But He was wounded for our transgressions, He was bruised for our guilt and iniquities; the chastisement [needful to obtain] peace and well-being for us was upon Him, and with the stripes [that wounded] Him we are healed and made whole." Isaiah 53:5 (AMP)

We have seen that Jesus gave the cup to His disciples and declared it to be His blood, shed to bring about the New Covenant. Now, compare the fourth cup on the table, where He saw His own shed blood and the anguish, the agony of His entire being that He would endure to bring the new covenant to pass. He must drink the cup and, in doing so, experience the suffering it contained. As we take the cup, He is giving to us His own shed blood—the same blood of His agony—but now releasing to us every blessing of the New Covenant, which fills us in totality: body, mind, emotions, and spirit. As we drink, we partake of the blessings, including the broad spectrum of healing.

The blood of Jesus was not shed at the cross! The Romans did not want their victims to die on the cross, but to suffer for days. Hanging Him on a cross was a public declaration to the world that He had been examined by a Roman court and found guilty of a heinous crime—a worthless sinner, fit only for death by crucifixion. The blood was shed during the scourging, which took place as a prelude to the agony of hanging on the cross. As we have seen, the scourging tore through muscles, exposed bone and organs, and ripped into arteries and veins, filling the shallow bath in which the scourging took place with blood.

It is significant that the Roman lash, with its pieces of jagged stone, sharp bone, and iron embedded in its leather thongs, was designed to rip apart *the back* of the victim. Every cell in our body is connected to the spine, and through it to the brain. By scourging His back, every organ in His body was immersed in pain. The scourging is noted as the place of healing—He bore every disease that fastened to every organ, through His shredded back!

Fear and anxiety take over the mind and emotions, repeating the message of doom like a mantra—over and over, around and around. Monotonous yet powerful, they amplify the sickness, threatening to carry its victim to death. But we partake of the Eucharist, which declares the Life that cannot be touched by death. From that meal of healing, go forth and arrest every thought that refuses to conform to this absolute truth.

> "For though we walk in the flesh, we do not war according to the flesh, for the weapons of our warfare are not of the flesh, but divinely powerful for the destruction of fortresses. We are destroying speculations, and every lofty thing raised up against the knowledge of God, and we are taking every thought captive to the obedience of Christ…" 2 Corinthians 10:3-5

We take every thought captive, arresting the empty speculations that rise up to contradict the truth of *"It is finished!"*

How do we do this? At the first sign of a message seeking entrance to our minds—whether it's sickness or failure in life—we counter it with the truth.

> "But if the Spirit of Him who raised Jesus from the dead dwells in you, He who raised Christ Jesus from the dead will also give life to your mortal bodies through His Spirit who dwells in you."
> Romans 8:11

This speaks to this present moment as we face this mental warfare that challenges who we are. Jesus, your New Covenant life, *gives life to our mortal bodies* through the Spirit within. It could not be plainer! We have a mortal body, but Christ in us means that we now share in His resurrection—the death-destroying life that, along with a host of other realities, collapses the power of sickness and silences the lie that would try to take over our minds. I known this from personal experience!

We do not live from one healing event to the next, but rather, we live drawing from His resurrection life with every breath. It is divine health rather than divine healing!

> "Therefore, whoever eats the bread or drinks the cup of the Lord in an unworthy manner, shall be guilty of the body and the blood of the Lord. But a man must examine himself, and in so doing he is to eat of the bread and drink of the cup. For he who eats and drinks, eats and drinks judgment

> to himself if he does not judge the body rightly. For this reason, many among you are weak and sick, and a number sleep. But if we judged ourselves rightly, we would not be judged. But when we are judged, we are disciplined by the Lord so that we will not be condemned along with the world." 1 Corinthians 11:27-32

This is a confusing and difficult verse, and I am not going to give an opinion as to the meaning of this entire passage, but that does not prevent us from getting to the heart of what Paul is saying here. Paul is telling us not to come to the Eucharist as if it were just any other meal, but to realize that something much deeper is happening here—something we should be aware of.

As we come to eat and drink, we examine ourselves. This does not mean that we come having dredged up every sin we can think of, approaching the meal in fear and religious terror!

I examine myself on a regular basis—meaning, I see myself as God has revealed that He sees me in Christ! I examine myself, remembering that Christ dwells in me, that He is my righteousness, and that I am beloved of the Father even as He is. To examine oneself apart from Christ, who is our life, is to deny His finished work and to present yourself in your own ragged attempts to be worthy. Examining oneself is a joyful, praise filled event, seeing that I am cleansed from all sin and am the delight of the Father!

If a person eats and drinks as if this is just common bread and wine, they fail to see the mystery and the wonder of what is taking place. To treat it as if it is a mere snack at the end of a service is to miss the reality that His broken body has absorbed and dismissed the judgment against sin for every human being. If we do not declare the *Amen* and revel in being one of mankind for whom He died and rose, then where do we turn for release from sin? How can you live if not from Christ in you, the One this bread and wine declare is your life?

Now we celebrate union with Christ—*you in Him and He in you!* The wonder of the New Covenant celebrates that your sins and iniquities are remembered no more! You are innocent through His blood! Your past sin is never to be rehearsed before the Father but instead, we give thanks for so great a salvation—a salvation that includes the healing of your mortal body!

Why would Paul say, "For this reason many among you are weak and sick, and a number have fallen asleep"? If you think this means that God goes through church killing people who did not "get it right," you need to hear the Good News! I believe Paul is saying that in partaking of the body and blood a river of life and healing is released. But to deny that, and treat it as a meaningless religious event, is to deny and miss the great blessing of healing for your entire person.

From this day forward, eat and drink the life of God in Christ and be healed—made whole for His glory!

14. Kinsman Redeemer

There is one other aspect of our life in Christ that we feast on in the Meal: we have been fully redeemed by His blood.

Ruth's story is set during the time of the Judges, likely around chapter 6, approximately 1,000 years before Jesus came. She enters the picture after Naomi and her husband, Elimilech, flee to Moab as refugees to escape a famine in Bethlehem, a small town in the tribe of Judah in Israel. The Moabites worshipped Chemosh, a demonized idol that demanded human sacrifices to be offered to gain its assistance. There was little or no love, kindness or respect of human life among such a people.

The first tragedy strikes shortly after they arrive— Elimilech dies, leaving Naomi a widow in a new, foreign land vastly different from where she came from. Despite this, she chooses to stay! Her two sons marry Moabite girls, Orpah and Ruth. But early in their marriages, both sons die, leaving Naomi alone once more. After ten years of sorrow and the darkening of her mind from living in such a harsh society, Naomi decides to return to Israel. Both of her two daughters-in-law initially insist on accompanying her. She persuades Orpah to stay, but Ruth insists on staying with her.

Ruth, a Moabite, would find it difficult moving to Israel. Born in a Chemosh-ruled society, she grew up aware of human sacrifices from an early age. She spoke a Moabite fashioned Hebrew which would be Hebrew with a strong accent and Canaanite words mixed in. This would make her stand out in a small community like Bethlehem. She crossed into Israel and came with Naomi to the town of Bethlehem in the tribe of Judah. Naomi was remembered and welcomed by the towns people, especially the older women. Ruth, however, would be viewed with suspicion, though nothing derogatory was said.

Although Naomi returned to her piece of land, she had been away ten years, and the house and buildings screamed of neglect and age. Doors creaked on ancient hinges, and the land resembled a jungle. This was a patriarchal society, and Naomi was alone—with no husband to support her—and the added responsibility of the dependent Moabite girl, Ruth, made the burden heavier. Naomi qualified for the welfare system of that day, which allowed her to go into the fields that were being harvested. As one of the town's poor, she was permitted to gather any barley or wheat that a clumsy reaper dropped, as they were forbidden by Law to pick it up. All carelessly dropped grain was to be left where it fell, for the poor to come and pick up. The same Law obligated farmers to leave the corners of their field untouched, allowing the poor to harvest those portions for themselves.

Naomi sent Ruth to join the group of girls who gathered in the early dawn to follow the harvesters. Those at the front of the line had first pickings of the dropped harvest. Ruth was accepted, though with some resentment—after all, she was a foreigner, taking food out of their mouths.

Later that morning Boaz—the owner of most of the fields—came to check on the progress of the harvest. He appears to have been told of this foreigner and her care of the older woman, Naomi. He sought Ruth out and welcomed her to the family of God's people. He privately told the harvesters who were working directly in front of her to be clumsy, dropping handfuls of barley for her to gather! His interest even went as far as having lunch with her. Something was stirring in Boaz toward the heavily accented girl from Moab.

The two women had an ample supply of food during the days of harvest, thanks to Boaz's secret instructions. But as harvest drew to an end they faced an empty food closet and no money to pay their bills. In Israel at that time, such a situation led to slavery as a way to pay off mounting debts—something two helpless woman could never hope to pay. While slavery provided food and shelter, it was still slavery.

A plan has been developing in Naomi's mind as Ruth came home each night with stories of Boaz' attention and kindness. Her plan was based on a custom in Israel designed for situations like theirs.

Naomi had been delighted when she learned that Ruth had unwittingly ended up in the fields of Boaz, the wealthy landowner. He was a brother of her dead husband. Such situations had been anticipated in the Law, which obligated a close relative to bail out a kinsman who was on the verge of losing their land due to unforeseen circumstances. This relative was called the *Goel,* meaning *kinsman-redeemer.* Another custom required the *Goel* to marry the widow, so the dead relative might have a son to carry on the family line.

The problem, however, was that Ruth was a Moabite. The villagers seem to have accepted her, but marrying her and bail her out was entirely different matter!

Naomi became the director of the plan, working in secret with Ruth each night. As the end of the harvest drew near, plans were made on the ranch to hold a party celebrating the harvest before winter. There would be no more gathering of the deliberate drops of barley until the next year. Naomi knew tonight was the night! She made sure Ruth is bathed, dressed in her best clothes, and instructed to wait until the party breaks up. Boaz, having had enough to drink, did not go home but slept in the barn, resting against a pile of grain. Following Naomi's instructions, Ruth came stealthily, lifted the blanket from the sleeping man's feet, and lay down there.

Boaz woke in the middle of the night, aware of the presence of someone curled up at his feet. Shocked and still half asleep, he called out, asking who was there. Ruth, as Naomi had taught her, responded "Cover me! For you are my *Goel*, my near kinsman."

Ruth had darker skin, but working all summer in the fields under the blazing sun had left her burned, with calloused and blistered hands. Her image of herself had plummeted, much like the Shulamite in the Song of Songs.

Boaz, however, was more than willing to fulfill his obligation—to bail out Naomi's land and take Ruth as his wife—but there was a complication: another man, a closer relative, and therefore a nearer *Goel*, had the first right of redemption ahead of Boaz. The matter would be settled at the city gates in the morning.

The elders of the city met daily at the gates to oversee such matters, and Boaz went there to alert them of his intentions. He waited until the nearer kinsman passed by, called him over, and presented his obligation to Naomi and her land. An astute businessman, seeing a financial opportunity, the man eagerly agreed, knowing he could pay off the debts, take over the land, and work it for profit. However, when Boaz introduced Ruth into the obligation, the nearest kinsman immediately withdrew. He refused to marry her—he had no interest in the person's involved, only in the potential financial gain from the land and its crops, perhaps even a few cattle.

The quaint custom that governed the exchange of property or relinquishing of one's rights to the property involved taking off the shoe of the person giving up their claim and handing it to the new owner, who assumed all rights to the property. Shoes symbolized control and ownership—the right to walk freely on land and exercise control of it. The man removed his shoe, signaling to everyone now gathered at the gates that he relinquished all rights to both the property, as well as to Naomi and Ruth. With this act,

Boaz can legally proceed to invest in the property and marry Ruth.

> Boaz married Ruth, and in the eyes of every Israelite, he brought her into his bloodline. Her Moabite lineage was now joined to and swallowed up in Boaz's lineage. Her very questionable genealogy was now made inseparably one with Boaz' which traced back to Abraham, the covenant promise, and the glorious future that God had sworn upon His Name to give.

Ruth did not know that she had already been included in that original promise! She was named as one of "*all the families of the earth*" who would be blessed with the covenant blessing of Abraham, and though her lineage wasn't pure, Moab was certainly one of the families of the earth!

The marriage vows and the feast that followed included the entire village. It was a day of changes bigger than most folk could comprehend, a feast of radical transformation affecting generations yet unborn. Death and resurrection were taking place in the laughing people whirling around in their ancient wedding dances.

Ruth, in fact died to her Moabite heritage, her family, and the controlling religion of Chemosh. This transformation begun in her commitment to Naomi as they crossed into Israel and was reaffirmed in the fields of Boaz. But marrying this man of faith and walking with him, learning from him, was her new trust in Yahweh.

Boaz also died to being sole owner of his vast ranch. It was talked about for years to come! The story was universally known, shared in every ale house between Jerusalem and the rolling hills of Zebulon and Naphtali. Boaz was now sharing his life, his ranch and all his possessions and abundant wealth with the Moabite girl. In his love for her, he gave himself to her without reserve.

Ruth found herself in a world she had never known! It wasn't just that she no longer had to think about unpaid bills and the threat of debtors' slavery—she was experiencing love for the first time. Moab knew nothing of love! Dominated by demons demanding human sacrifice on a regular basis, there was little to no room for self-giving love, compassion, care, or kindness among the populace, even in marriages and family life. For Ruth, to be assured of the love of Boaz, to see his eyes admiring her, proud of her beauty—he didn't see her as a sunburnt field worker, but as a beautiful lady who stirred his heart and made him proud. In his gaze, he bestowed upon her worth and a new kind of beauty. His look made her know acceptance, giving her a new identity that she began to adjust to. She was baptized into a new world, one characterized by a love that flowed from Yahweh.

All the bills and threats of slavery now landed on Boaz's desk, no longer on Naomi's kitchen table. The debt collectors who once hammered on their door fell back when Boaz appeared in the doorway! Their presence, their fistful of bills carried no threat or fear, they simply disappeared—his wealth swallowed them up!

Ruth no longer walked through town with downcast eyes, avoiding the looks of disdain directed at *the Moabite who had lived off our welfare*. Now, she walked with her head held high, greeted by all as the wife of Boaz. She shared his honor and respect. She knew that to disrespect her would be disrespect to him.

The property had been a mess! The young girl had spent all summer in the fields with the poor, working daily from sunup to sundown. There had been no time to repair broken sheds, fix doors, or tend a house on the verge of collapse. Naomi, too old and feeble to help with repairs, sat in the middle of the mess, requiring all of Ruth's time to care for her and prepare the food.

Boaz inherited the broken buildings, and neglected land, but his servants transformed it within a week, turning the jungle into a garden of beauty, the same as the gardens at his own mansion.

> Both the groom and the bride died that day of the wedding, and both rose from that death as the two who had become the new one.

Soon, they had a son, and Ruth's great-grandson was Jesse, the father of David, with whom God made a covenant—a covenant that continued the covenant with Abraham. The line of Ruth and Boaz, through David, ended in Mary's womb with Jesus!!

Boaz was kinsman-redeemer because he was close kin, wealthy enough to meet the challenge, and able to cover Naomi and Ruth in their time of need. He loved Ruth as she was, elevating the situation beyond a mere legal matter, that would say with a sigh, "It is my obligation, I must take her," to love that declared with delight said, "I want her!" Boaz died that she might live. The owner of all became one with the field girl—rough hands, sunburnt skin, and all. He became one with the woman who picked what was dropped and left behind to survive another next day. He died to his abundance and took on her poverty, exchanging her experience of poverty with his wealth and abundance

> She was redeemed from life under Chemosh. Redeemed from poverty, dishonor, disrespect. At the heart of it all was his personal, intimate love for her—a love she had never known before—the attributes of *Agape*.

The love Boaz had for Ruth, which he declared publicly, bestowed on her a worth far beyond mere dollar value. It was the worth his love placed on her, and that value transferred to all who saw it. They now loved, honored, and befriended her, seeing and knowing her through Boaz's eyes. But that change was not automatic—Ruth must participate in the wonders taking place around her and to her. Is it possible for a poor person to become rich? True riches are not something recorded in a bank account! Poverty is a mindset, a way of thinking, a perspective on life and future expectations, not something determined by a bank balance. Poverty speaks from within, "I am not, I have not and I will not have" and even with vast material possessions, poverty will keep on dictating life from within.

> Boaz's love placed a worth on Ruth, bestowed a value beyond all the money now at her disposal. His love taught her to say, "I have, and I am. I will have enough, and I will always be enough!"

Wealth was not in counting her cash or being satisfied she had more pennies than anyone else in Bethlehem. In fact, I doubt she ever bothered to count it! Ruth simply knew—she thought in terms of abundance and accepted the reality of being one with Boaz. There was no more fear of loss, no fear of not having enough, and no dread of the knock on the door from debt collectors. Boaz did not see her as the separated Moabite, but as one with him, *his beloved Ruth*.

She was not ashamed to think of herself as someone who could say, "I have enough and more to spare. I can and I will…" This was the atmosphere she now lived in—an atmosphere she could taste and revel in. This attitude to life, the life of abundance did not make her feel awkward; love filled the place where fear once reigned. The life she had left behind, the one that died the day of her marriage, had dictated "You are supposed to be fearful." Friends from those old days dismissed her as having become proud! She was no longer of their kind! She was no longer ashamed of the consciousness of "I have, I can." She had a new identity—no longer the Moabite, but the wife of Boaz.

Knowing herself as beloved, she discovered who she truly was. She must live on purpose, deliberately, with intention grounded in Boaz's love and wealth. She no longer sang, "I'm only a Moabite saved by grace," or "I'm not perfect, just a Moabite married to Boaz".

Few people realize that *God took upon Himself the title of Goel—the Kinsman-Redeemer, the Restorer.* Most of our Bible translations have it simply as Redeemer (which is wonderful enough!). However, the Passion translation has correctly translated as Kinsman-Redeemer.

> "But now, thus says the Lord, your Creator, O Jacob, and He who formed you, O Israel, "Do not fear, for I have redeemed you; I have called you by name; you are Mine! When you pass through the waters, I will be with you; and through the rivers, they will not overflow you. When you walk through the fire, you will not be scorched, nor will the flame burn you. For I am the Lord your God, the Holy One of Israel, your Savior… Since you are precious in My sight, since you are honored, and I love you… Do not fear, for I am with you…" Isaiah 43:1-7

When He says "I have redeemed you," He is declaring, "I am your Kinsman-Redeemer, and I have redeemed you."

This anticipated the Incarnation when God would become flesh—a true member of the human family, our brother, Kinsman Redeemer—without ceasing to be God. God became our kin; human blood flowed in His veins, but that blood was *the blood of God*.

> "In Him we have redemption through His blood, the forgiveness of our trespasses, according to the riches of His grace which He lavished on us." Ephesians 1:7-8

In Him, our Kinsman Redeemer, consider the worth He has bestowed on us, "… riches of His grace which He lavished on us." To 'lavish' includes a pouring out and over us, soaking us in grace that superabounds. When preaching in Africa, the natives picked up on what I was teaching and their way of expressing it was "His grace is plenty too much!"

> "For you know the grace of our Lord Jesus Christ, that though He was rich, yet for your sake He became poor, so that you through His poverty might become rich." 2 Corinthians 8:9-10

> "For you are becoming progressively acquainted with and recognizing more strongly and clearly the grace of our Lord Jesus Christ (His kindness, His gracious generosity, His undeserved favor and spiritual blessing), [in] that though He was [so very] rich, yet for your sakes He became [so very] poor, in order that by His poverty you might become enriched (abundantly supplied)." 2 Corinthians 8:9-10 (AMP)

The Holy Spirit opens our eyes to see that our true and vast value is in His love for us! His suffering and blood shedding are the lengths He will go to, to bring us into the abundance of life and provision we were created for. This includes everything He took to Himself in the incarnation: our limitless knowing of the Trinity, a clear mind receiving revelation from the Spirit, deliverance from all fears and anxiety, now filled with His love. It means being saved from fleeting happiness and receiving enduring joy and peace beyond human comprehension. It also involves our physical lives on this planet and our bodies kept in divine health. We come to realize and take hold all of this as our own as we partake of the Meal of New Covenant.

The one with first right to the property and Ruth is very much like *the Law*. The Law is a faceless stranger, seeing humans as outsiders beneath his class, with no love or compassion for Ruth or any of us. It seeks only clear title to the property, discarding Ruth as an unsuitable Moabite, unable to meet its standards for marriage. She is fit only for accusations and judgment!

But Jesus, joined with us in an unbreakable, inseparable union dies our death—separating us from the world of sin and death. In dying for us, and as us, He raises us from that death to live in Him for the rest of time and eternity. Together we are in the Father.

> He joyfully takes the mess of our lives and beautifies us with His love, shed abroad in our hearts.

As for the Law, it has no claim over us. At the cry of victory, *"It is finished"*, it submits, handing over the shoe—relinquishing all rights to you! You are redeemed by the blood of Jesus, your slate wiped clean by his unending love for you! The Law has handed the shoe-right concerning you to Jesus, and it is recorded in the Father's court that it has no authority to step into your life or make even the slightest accusation concerning you.

In Deuteronomy, there is a law somewhat similar, but with a key difference: the rejected woman was to take the shoe and spit in the face of the man who refused to have compassion on her. Now, it is time for many to fully embrace Jesus-Boaz love and acceptance and take away the shoe—declaring that the Law has no more place in your life! It legally cannot walk back in your life. Spit in the face of the Law if it dares to open its accusing mouth, cutting off all discussion and any thought of giving it a foothold.

15. Christ As Us

There is much confusion over the work of Christ in our Western church. The question, in its simplest terms, is: *"How did Jesus save us? How did He bring about our salvation?"* This brings the second question: *"What do we experience taking place when we participate in the body and blood of Christ in our hand?"*

David, living 1,000 years before Christ, was a prophet who spoke of Him by expressing His feelings and thoughts—His experience of life—through his own! In the story of David facing Goliath, we are brought to the heart of what was happening in Jesus being our Savior.

David was an Israelite, descendant of Abraham. When he went to face the gigantic Philistine, Goliath, he was standing as his extended family, his kinfolk. Although rejected as too young to fight in King Saul's army, he quickly made himself heard, first to his brothers and then the circle of their friends. This battle demanded that whoever went to fight Goliath would represent not only the army but all of Israel. Saul, the king, could not send an urgent message to some trained special forces or mercenaries from a nearby country, like Edom, asking them to send one of the descendants of Esau to stand in for Israel and fight Goliath. It would not work—they were of the wrong genealogy, raised in the wrong country.

David did not fit the image of Israel's representative for this battle with Goliath, but working with sheep, unknown in the hills around Bethlehem, he not only had the pedigree—a family tree that was impeccable, going directly back to Abraham—but also carried a secret: a destiny and a calling to care for Israel just as he cared for his father's sheep. Samuel the prophet had visited the ranch and already anointed David to be the next king of Israel. He was the first ***messiah***, a Hebrew word meaning 'the anointed' or 'one smeared with oil,' upon whom the Spirit came, enabling him to be prepared for the time when he would lead the people of Israel to victory over all who sought to take their land from them. Through this young teenager, and over a thousand years of descendants, Jesus was born of the line of David to rescue and restore Israel and all families of the earth to their original status at creation as the image bearers of God.

> Later, Israel spoke of being joined to David, as if they were part of him, just as he was part of them. His history from the beginning was woven together with theirs—although only he knew that!

It was a local war fought over land that brought this into stark focus. The Philistines, a seagoing folk, were in search of land to call home base. Their longboats cut through the water—whether under sail or rowed against the wind—bore the carved, ugly image of their god carved into the front of the boat. The villagers living in their shacks along the waterfront prayed they would never see the silhouette of the sails against the horizon or an ugly pagan face pulling into the harbor.

The Philistines had already established themselves along the southwestern beaches of Israel, but they were hungry for more land and so they had begun moving inland. King Saul called all men of fighting age to assemble to protect their land. The call to war came to the ranch of Jesse and he sent his eldest sons to battle. David—the youngest, the misunderstood, rejected by the family and the one sent to the hills to shepherd the sheep — stayed at home. He was in the range of 14 or 15 years old.

The parallel to Jesus is arresting. Jesus, the direct descendant of David, carried the weight of a destiny that no one knew of except His parents—though they would find it difficult to put into words. His call went back to before creation, when the Trinity determined to create, and specifically to create the human in Their image and likeness. It was determined that the Son of God would take on human flesh and become human. The Creator would take to Himself all mankind; assuming their history, would bring them into His own history, making them sons of God in and with Him, the Son. He became flesh, and no one knew who He was. He came to His own people and kinfolk, and they did not recognize the identity of the One who lived, played, and studied among them.

His mission was to become one with the human condition, to know the human from the inside, and to take it upon Himself, carrying it through death to resurrection and to the life intended from before time.

David was sent by his father with gifts for his fighting brothers and to bring back news of the battle. What no one outside of the battle knew was that it had reached a shameful stalemate. The Philistine army was of an average height. They wore brass battle dress and fought with the sun shining full on their polished armor, blinding the eyes of the opposing army and making them appear twice their size. Among them, however, was a family twice as large as everyone else. When they put on their armor, radiant in the sunlight, they were terrifying to behold. Goliath was of that family.

He didn't need to be a great fighter! He only had to show up and bully his victims. In full armor, completely covered with brass, he was safe from any thrown spears. Using his size, he would lumber to the front lines and throw the challenge: he would fight one of the Hebrews, and the winner took all. Why waste many lives when two people could fight and end the war with a single defeat? It sounded like good sense—if you were Goliath! He walked the length of Israel's lines, mocking and shouting his challenge. He did this at breakfast and at supper, making sure Israel woke up to hear it and went to bed hearing it. Goliath had kept this up relentlessly for six weeks, filling their days and haunting their dreams.

Into this camp, David arrived fresh from the hills, where he looked upon his sheep as a sacred mission and understood life as a seamless union with God—something few in the Old Testament knew anything of. The LORD, Yahweh, was his life and strength. He assumed that all of Israel knew their privilege and identity as the covenant people of God, and would have, in His strength, protected their land, then been ready to come home. Instead, he arrived in the camp only to face a wall of fear, unbelief, and the shame of their cowardice.

David arrived early in the morning as Goliath was sending his message across the army of Israel. He didn't know they had been hearing this for six weeks, now moving into week seven. He thought it was the first time and waited expectantly for one of his brothers to jump to the challenge. He sensed the despair, hopelessness clinging to the soldiers like a thick fog. The camp was engulfed in the darkness of death and futility, believing that they could do nothing to stop this monster at their door. 'I am not… I cannot… none of us can' was the sick air they breathed.

David took the situation in, and though being mocked by his brothers and seen as a curiosity by many, he continued to speak in terms of the power of Yahweh to overcome Goliath and crush these pagans. David initiated the meeting with Goliath in the Valley of Elah, which lay between the two armies. No one volunteered him for the task. No one sat him down to tell him it was his duty. He now knew why he had come that morning. He must stop this mockery of the God he knew as his closest friend and true life. He was smiled at as someone slightly deranged, jeered at, and mocked by his brothers. Israel had come to the place where they believed Goliath. Somewhere in the last two months, they had accepted Goliath's mindset as their own. From that day, Goliath owned Israel, and both sides awaited the inevitable day of Israel's death and defeat. Here stood a mere boy who did not believe that—a boy who believed what God believed!

Jesus was rejected as the Messiah, and His mission as the joke of religion, whether the Temple or the local Pharisee. Yet, He never wavered from the reason the Father sent Him or the cost that would demand: bloodshed and death. He believed His Father would raise Him from the dead. He came to deliver mankind from the Liar Serpent, the Dragon monster that held mankind in fear. Similarly, King Saul, who should have led the troops, interviewed David, and seeing his determination, offered an official send-off by giving him his armor. David refuses the armor as useless to him. Just as Satan came to Jesus more than once, urging Him to take the methods of this world to accomplish His mission—'Get the allegiance of the people by feeding them, performing miracle stunts, or putting on a religious circus. Let them crown You king and go in military force—but do not go to do this work as a weak, helpless, unprotected human being.'

David did not approach Saul with plans to mediate a cease fire or 'manage' Goliath—he wasn't a U.N. peace force. He came to rid the earth of the monstrous creature. He had one plan, with no contingency! This young boy announced that he would walk into death—for by now, every soldier believed that stepping out of the camp into the valley was stepping into death. Yet, he was sure he would return with Goliath's head, delivering the people and restoring peace.

David stood in the place of every Israelite—not only every soldier who had their eyes glued on him, but multi-thousands who hardly knew there was a war! He stood for the elderly, sitting in their cottages, herding the sun across the sky, who might never know there was a war, let alone a champion who finished it with one blow! *In these moments, David became Israel.* He was not doing something for Israel to later decide whether they would accept it or not. He would come out of death the conqueror, victorious by his faith in Yahweh, and declare to the people that they were no longer under oppression.

Jesus, the substance of which David had been the shadow, told His closest friends that they could not come with Him—that He alone would bring this to pass. In that cosmic moment, He became all. No one, not even His closest friends, knew what He was doing; they would be the first to know, but as He entered the Valley of Death, they fled from Him—terrified and confused—sure they would never see Him again. Millions sat in their homes and cottages not knowing the end of the world had come and, in the same breath, its resurrection—and all centered in the One Man who, in Himself, overthrew the Serpent Dragon and is the beginning of the New Creation. Those millions would find out one day what He did, but not on the day He went into Death and brought it down.

> Jesus began by establishing new rules—the Serpent was not in control; it never had been! As they came to arrest Him, He spoke two words and everyone fell on their back, helpless. He used the rage of His captors to enter their raging, fear-filled hearts. His blood they shed would be the blood that cleansed them from all sin.

Standing before King Saul and surveying the valley of death, David ***remembered*** the lion and the bear that had attacked his sheep. In the name of Yahweh, he had killed them both! It is noteworthy that he did not remember failures but saw ***all his history*** as a triumph of God's ongoing purpose.

David received no help from the soldiers sitting behind him as he walked to the valley. Yet, he received what they did not know they were giving. Looking at him with pity, seeing a bright-eyed boy with great ideas, they believed they would never see him again! In their glances, they sent him their fear, their sneering laugh, and their unbelief—their great sin against the God of covenant with them, who had committed to be their defense. David went into the valley clothed in their shame, unbelief, and their sin of having forgotten who they were because they had forgotten who their God was.

He was clothed in their fear, but he never succumbed to it. Then he was met with the intensely dark mindset and imagination of Goliath that descended on him like a spider web, but David never yielded an inch to it. When he slew Goliath, not only the giant would die, but the entire sinful, negative mindset that found its existence in him. All Israel would walk into the valley that day, and their fear and shame would die with Goliath, who had given it oxygen. A new Israel would rise, instantly reborn, as David emerged from the valley holding death by its forelock!

Jesus, in His sufferings, took upon Himself the sin of the world; He became sin for us. Our fear of not knowing who God truly is, of not knowing who we were, and therefore failing to be who we were created to be—all the darkness, corruption, and shame of humanity—He became. He forgave us all and dismissed the sin, giving us instead His mind and all He is.

It is important to note that David's driving force was to remove the one who mocked, defied, and held captive the people who belonged to God. Goliath had dragged the glory of God through the mud and mocked Him. *David came to reveal the name of God—who He truly is, the God they have forgotten—and in so doing, set the people free*. His mission was not solely to free the people or to bring them blessing. 'Goliath, you do not realize that Yahweh is not a local god that can be messed with! In His Name you will lose your headship this day.'

Jesus, God in flesh, came to crush the head of the serpent and let the glory of God be known—God revealing God's love at its most glorious moment of first loving us when we were at our worst. To glorify God is to reveal Him as good as truly He is!

> "Father, the hour has come; glorify Your Son, that the Son may glorify You… I glorified You on the earth, having accomplished the work which You have given Me to do. Now, Father, glorify Me together with Yourself, with the glory which I had with You before the world was." John 17:1-5

> "O righteous Father, although the world has not known You, yet I have known You; and these have known that You sent Me; and I have made Your name known to them, and will make it known, so that the love with which You loved Me may be in them, and I in them." John 17:25-26

As Goliath fell, and David hacked off his head with the giant sword, he did this *as Israel*—not as mere spectators, neither sitting in the bleachers that morning watching the show nor reading it as a distant event of history years later. By the faith of God, he had brought down the monster and the entire Empire of Darkness that had come to make their home there. As Israel's army—who had fled before Goliath for nearly seven weeks—saw him defeated, David's faith entered them. They leaped from where they stood into the valley, sending the Philistine army fleeing before them. David had mirrored a man of faith to them, sending the message, 'This is who every one of you truly is!' They heard and, in moments, became a mighty army.

Israel's army shouted, congratulating themselves and David, seeing themselves one with him—their histories entwined, and their identity as one seamless, inseparable, spontaneous union, living relationship in action. "We are not sitting watching him do something *for us* but feeling *the divine excitement and emotion because it was and is all as us*." They ran to finish off the Philistines *with David's legs under them.*

> Jesus did this *as us*—we are not mere spectators looking into the window of ancient history.

He tells us, "This is you; our histories unite." He takes our death, and we take His life. We give our bondage and fears, and He gives us His deliverance and restoration. Jesus mirrored, "This is who we are." *Metanoia* is seeing as He sees and knowing ourselves to be who He says we are.

No soldier, prince, or king could boast of his involvement in bringing down Goliath. They saw this faith operate in David, and as they did, they trusted the God of that faith, and became strong. Only the *faith of God* could bring down the entire Empire of Death and darkness, and Jesus is the faith of God in our humanity: "He is the Author and Finisher of our faith." That faith delivers us, and through the Spirit, becomes our faith by which we live, abide, and bring forth the life of Christ in our world.

> *Jesus is the Savior, not us!!* He does not produce a thing called salvation—He becomes our sin and is Himself our Savior. Salvation is not a product, but a dynamic relationship, *life in Christ.*

Jesus went alone into Death, *dying for us by dying as us,* and in so doing every human is included into His salvation. He went with all their belief in the Lie that they were separated from God even though it was the greatest lie of the master who controlled them. He personally took all our fears, our rank unbelief in the faithfulness of God, our willful blindness to our identity as God's covenant people, and our addiction to listening to the voice of the Satan and turning a deaf ear to the God of covenant love—all of our despair, futility, and hopelessness weighed on His back. He went *as* them, *as* us, carrying our wretchedness in His body to Death on the cross. He did not go just to do something for us, but *as us*—we look and see ourselves in His face.

> "He made Him who knew no sin to be sin
> on our behalf, so that we might
> become the righteousness of God in
> Him." 2 Corinthians 5:21

> "I am crucified with Christ: nevertheless I
> live; yet not I, but Christ liveth in me:
> and the life which I now live in the

> flesh I live by the faith of the Son of God, who loved me, and gave himself for me." Galatians 2:20 (KJV)

> "With Christ I have been crucified, and live no more do I, and Christ doth live in me; and that which I now live in the flesh – in the faith I live of the Son of God, who did love me and did give himself for me." Galatians 2:20 (YLT98)

David went into the valley of death that promised death to everyone that would dare to enter, and inside he overcame the threatened death and destroyed the one, who until then, held the power of death. His victory is a shadow image of what finally took place in Jesus *as us,* entering our death and, in the resurrection, bringing an end to death ruling mankind.

> "...Do not be afraid; I am the first and the last, and the living One; and I was dead, and behold, I am alive forevermore, and I have the keys of death and of Hades." Revelation 1:17-18

> "Therefore, since the children share in flesh and blood, He Himself likewise also partook of the same, that through death He might render powerless him who had the power of death, that is, the devil, and might free those who through fear of death were subject to

> slavery all their lives." Hebrews 2:14-15

Jesus *overcame death by entering death as us, as human, bearing our sin,* and *from inside death, He destroys death, as shown in His resurrection.* He became our sin, and then became our death before becoming our life that cannot die.

Every demon and power of darkness saw this and knows it to this day and flees in terror, as did the Philistines.

Goliath is beheaded. Death is dead. It is Jesus throwing aside the stone at the door of the tomb and walking out free from the burden He carried in. His mangled body, torn by the sin of the world, is now smooth, healed, and whole! He has taken away the sin of the world; He is free from our burden. The entirety of mankind walked out with Him, for *He did this as us. Faith is not a work but the response to and resting in Another's work.*

> "And although you were formerly alienated and hostile in mind, engaged in evil deeds, yet He has now reconciled you in His fleshly body through death, in order to present you before Him holy and blameless and beyond reproach." Colossians 1:21-22

> "Your indifferent mindset alienated you from God into a lifestyle of annoyances, hardships, and labors. Yet he has now fully reconciled and restored

> you to your original design. He accomplished this in dying our death in a human body; he fully represented us in order to fully present us again in blameless innocence, face-to-face with God…" Colossians 1:21-22a (Mirror Bible)

David's victory was accomplished before Israel moved—they had nothing to do with it except move within it and enjoy its authority as they left their seats of fear and ran into the valley of death, shouting the victory that now filled the air. How many fall in our modern church because they have been taught that the victory is to be won or lost based on their faith, their prayer, and their witnessing. They face their own helplessness and fall, only to be condemned for being weak and backsliding.

Falling down becomes normal in a world where eyes are riveted on oneself as the source of salvation—asking, "Have I done enough? Am I strong enough?"—identifying with poverty and 'cannot' failure, so that falling feels right and normal. When eyes are focused only on Jesus as the Savior and Life, we accept our weakness as the container of Him and draw from His strength. When we answer these questions with expectancy in Jesus, everything we believe is challenged, and only the truth will emerge, new and working in our lives.

In the Eucharist, we eat and drink of Him, participating in the risen Christ, living by His faith, with eyes continually opened to see that this is the way things are—we say the Amen to His

Person. This is a feast of exultation, the great, wild thanksgiving. Galatians 2:20—our entire life is 'in Christ, in us.'

16. Participation

Paul was the persecutor of the first believers until Jesus met him when he was on his way to persecute believers in Damascus. Many of those he had persecuted had been with Jesus in Galilee and were firsthand witnesses of His miracles and teaching. Paul's dramatic life change became one of the great wonders of the early church, but he lacked the personal experience that the other leaders of the church had with Jesus. This left him at a disadvantage compared to the other apostles, as he knew nothing of the life and teachings of Jesus.

He did not receive the understanding and implications of the Gospel from the apostles. The fact is, they were not too welcoming when he first came among them as a new convert—they feared that his conversion might be a ploy to get firsthand knowledge of the whereabouts of the believers! Paul then went away and there is a period during which we know very little about his whereabouts or what he was doing. It was during those years that the Holy Spirit revealed to him not only the Gospel but a depth of understanding that surpassed that of the twelve apostles. Paul received a revelation that unveiled the vastness of the meaning: Christ is in us, and we are in Him. He shared this unique insight, taught to him by the Spirit, in his letters. Ephesians 3 is his testimony of receiving the gift of that revelation.

> "For this reason I, Paul, the prisoner of Christ Jesus for the sake of you Gentiles—if indeed you have heard of the stewardship of God's grace which was given to me for you; that by revelation there was made known to me the mystery, as I wrote before in brief. By referring to this, when you read you can understand my insight into the mystery of Christ, which in other generations was not made known to the sons of men, as it has now been revealed to His holy apostles and prophets in the Spirit; to be specific, that the Gentiles are fellow heirs and fellow members of the body, and fellow partakers of the promise in Christ Jesus through the gospel, of which I was made a minister, according to the gift of God's grace which was given to me according to the working of His power. To me, the very least of all saints, this grace was given, to preach to the Gentiles the unfathomable riches of Christ, and to bring to light what is the administration of the

mystery which for ages has been
hidden in God who created all things;
so that the manifold wisdom of God
might now be made known through
the church to the rulers and the
authorities in the heavenly places.
This was in accordance with the
eternal purpose which He carried out
in Christ Jesus our Lord, in whom we
have boldness and confident access
through faith in Him...

"For this reason I bow my knees before the
Father, from whom every family in
heaven and on earth derives its name,
that He would grant you, according to
the riches of His glory, to be strength-
ened with power through His Spirit in
the inner man, so that Christ may
dwell in your hearts through faith; and
that you, being rooted and grounded in
love, may be able to comprehend with
all the saints what is the breadth and
length and height and depth, and to
know the love of Christ which
surpasses knowledge, that you may be
filled up to all the fullness of God.
Now to Him who is able to do far
more abundantly beyond all that we
ask or think, according to the power
that works within us, to Him be the
glory in the church and in Christ Jesus
to all generations forever and ever.
Amen." Ephesians 3:1-21

This revelation was not in a vacuum, detached from what others were saying. It is often overlooked that Paul includes the Eucharist in the revelation the Spirit taught him. *Everything we find in his epistles was to be understood against the backdrop of the Eucharist.* It is amazing that Paul was the first to write down what happened that night in Jerusalem when Jesus instituted the meal—even though he was not there! His detailed account of what happened is used in many churches to this day when celebrating the Eucharist! He wrote it down before the Gospel accounts of Matthew, Mark, and Luke were written.

He began his account of Jesus instituting the Eucharist with the words, "*I received of the Lord* what I passed on to you…" The celebration of this Holy Communion was not a take-it-or-leave-it or optional add-on to the great spiritual truth Paul was given—it was a necessary part of that revelation! *This meal is of such importance that the entire revelation of Christ in us required the revelation of the Eucharist to be fully understood!*

This is not a meal directed at feeding our intellect; this is not a Bible study but experiencing Him alive in our hearts. Consider the two disciples on their way home along the Emmaus Road, after witnessing the devastation of the crucifixion. Jesus comes up alongside them under the guise of a traveler. After noticing their faces reflecting utter despair, He questions them, and then leads them in a Bible study through the Old Testament, explaining the Messiah's expected suffering. They reported later that as He spoke and opened the Scriptures, *"our hearts burned within us!"*

Upon arriving in Emmaus, they convinced Him to come in for supper. When seated, He took the bread and broke it, and suddenly, they realize they are in a Eucharist and He is the risen Christ, celebrating at their table! Reporting that happening later, they exclaimed, "*He was made known to us in the breaking of the bread!*"

The promises wrapped in the New Covenant are now experienced through the Holy Spirit. This is the blood that reconciles mankind to the God they have rejected. It brings us to Him, assuring each one of us that we can now call Him Father, Abba. It cleanses us from all sin, washing and making the unclean righteous. It redeems our lives from the poverty of soul, imprisoned in the darkness of the lie, and heals from the sickness of body, emotions, and mind, cleansing the entire person from sin. It infuses those shattered by grief and sorrow with divine comfort. It shouts the good news to all that through this bloodshed, we have acceptance with the Father, Son, and Spirit; our shame is gone with all sin consciousness and cowering fear.

We are not called to intellectual knowledge, to merely knowing about Him. If that were the case, He would have given us a Bible, placed us in a study or a library, and given us the identity of a student. Instead, He gave us a meal: bread, wine, a setting usually in the kitchen, with an identity as hungry persons enjoying a relationship, friends rejoicing, thankful at a meal.

> He calls it *the cup of blessing which we bless.* This identifies it as the third cup of the Passover table.

The context of the meal takes us back to where we began in John 6. The chapter opens with the feeding of the five thousand, followed by a conversation arising about the manna—God's gift of food provided over a forty-year period in the wilderness led by

Moses. It was the miracle food; they didn't know what it was and therefore called it *manna*, meaning 'what is it' in Hebrew! It nourished every man, woman, and child in Israel, providing everything they needed. It appeared under the desert mist every morning, except on the Sabbath day of rest. Jesus presented Himself as our true food, the ultimate Manna—the Bread of Life.

Let me underscore the fact this is not addressing our intellect. When we come to eat and drink, we do so in the 'is' of faith in Him, who serves us with this 'is' My body, this 'is' My blood, and we are plunged into the wonder of the new covenant. We cannot grasp with our intellect that He dwells within us, and we in Him! We live our life *'is-ing'* Christ our life. Do not debate—eat and drink!

We are not told to try to think or imagine it, because it is beyond our mental process. It is physical faith. We are to physically do it, and He does it with us. It is not about begging or groveling with a religious whine. The command "Take, eat" indicates a bold taking of that which we know to be ours.

He said, "As often as you do…" which speaks of repetition. Why do many celebrate every week? Jesus gave no limit—so why repetition? This is the most important experience in our personal and corporate lives—relationship today with the ascended Christ. This is not a family reunion once every five years! *We do not set time aside once a year with our loved one! This* celebration is the remembrance of all remembrances—by '*do this in remembrance of Me,'* we are bringing heaven into the middle of the chaos of earth and adjusting our view of life, settling into the remembrance taking place in front of us. This is the continual adjusting our vision to truth.

The repetition is not 'vain,' empty doing or saying things mechanically by rote. It is the way of Biblical meditation set forth in the entire Scripture. The word 'meditation' in Hebrew means 'chew the cud,'—to do and redo until it governs the way you think, speak, and act. It carries the resultant memorization to the person, who now mutters and talks about what is being revealed—not what one ought to do or try to do, not a list of rules, but plunging into what is being said or done, knowing at the deepest level that *'this is so and is now at work in me.'* Constantly revisiting the Eucharist creates an atmosphere in the fellowship that one could not produce by teaching or prayer meetings!

I came to Christ among Pentecostals and spent many years ministering with the charismatic movement. The movement reflected my experience of the Spirit and His giftings, but I had a problem with their understanding of freedom and liberty. Liberty, for many of those folk, meant never doing or saying the same thing twice—new and different described liberty in the Spirit. I am ready for the Spirit to do a new thing, but I am also ready to follow the believers over the last two thousand plus years and let them teach me how some services have been conducted for most of those two thousand years.

When I know what is going to be done and said, I am at liberty to enjoy the moment, set free from the 'how' it will be done. As I write this, in a few weeks, it will be Thanksgiving here in the US. We do not discuss the menu! If it had changed in the last fifty years, it would upset the entire day! What we will do is also set, leaving us free from decision making so we can celebrate as it has been done from the beginning. One could be foolish for a moment and say that it's so settled, there's no point of discussion —that we will eat at a table with knives and forks, not on the floor with grape leaves to celebrate our freedom! This year, the ladies have decided to cook in the oven in the kitchen rather than on the wood fire at the end of the garden! These decisions, passed down from grandmothers to grandchildren, do not restrict us but instead free us to fully celebrate the day.

We celebrate the Eucharist following the pattern of the church since the beginning, allowing us to revel in the love of God in Christ. And knowing who He is, we know who we are in Him. As the truth sinks deeper into the recesses of our heart, we find we are changing and learning how to rest in Christ. We often have people drop by our fellowship to see what we are about, and afterward, come to ply me with questions. My answer comes down to this: *"Come and join us with an open heart for twelve weeks, and then see if you can leave! I believe you will have become accustomed to what the Spirit is doing in the Eucharist and will find it difficult, if not impossible, to walk away."*

We mentioned Paul receiving a revelation that is the subject of most of the epistles, and it is also lived out in the weekly partaking of the body and blood of Christ. He also had revelation of what was takes place when we come together to eat and drink of His body and blood:

> "*Is not the cup of blessing which we bless a sharing in the blood of Christ? Is not the bread which we break a sharing in the body of Christ?* Since there is one bread, we

who are many are one body; for we all partake of the one bread… are not those who eat the sacrifices sharers in the altar? What do I mean then? That a thing sacrificed to idols is anything, or that an idol is anything? No but I say that the things which the Gentiles sacrifice, *they sacrifice to demons and not to God; and I do not want you to become sharers in demons*. You cannot drink the cup of the Lord and the cup of demons; you cannot partake of the table of the Lord and the table of demons. Or do we provoke the Lord to be jealous? We are not stronger than He, are we?" 1 Corinthians 10:16-22

"When we drink the cup of blessing, aren't we taking into ourselves the blood, the very life, of Christ? And isn't it the same with the loaf of bread we break and eat? Don't we take into ourselves the body, the very life, of Christ? Because there is one loaf, our many-ness becomes one-ness — Christ doesn't become fragmented in us. Rather, we become unified in him. We don't reduce Christ to what we are; he raises us to what he is." 1 Corinthians 10:16 (MSG)

Paul refers to the Corinthians as 'wise' or 'sensible' people, and they can understand what he is about to say. This suggests that, although the text doesn't explicitly mention it, these believers likely celebrated the Eucharist regularly, equipping them with insight into the significance of his teachings.

In the idol temples, offerings were sacrificed to the various gods that the pagans worshiped, but these gods were empty, make-believe, nothings! Yet behind these empty, dead gods, these people had opened themselves to real demonic powers. To eat at the meals in the temples was to become a sharer, partaker, of those demon forces. How much more, then, to partake of the cup of the blood of Christ and eat of His body, becoming a partaker of the living Christ! That statement lifts the Eucharist out of the realm of merely an aid to the memory of an historical Christ *to the radiant presence of Christ here and now, present and uniting Himself with us as we eat and drink.*

> Take another look at 1 Corinthians 10:16. As we drink of the cup, *we share in and participate in fellowship, communion, being with, and in partnership with Christ's blood.*

We are not remembering ancient history; we are not at the wake of the dead Christ, trying to conjure up images from His history in the Gospels. Instead, we are participating in the effects, in this moment, of the living body and blood of the risen Christ.

Participation can only take place when we are actively taking part in something that is now happening. One *participates* in sports, in a game currently taking place in real-time, or we *participate* in a discussion where we speak, question, or offer opinions. We cannot participate in something that happened last year—or 2000 years ago! We do not participate in pictures of an event!

Participation means that we are there, experiencing and engaging our emotions and intellect. We experience, taste what is taking place, knowing despair or elation—the experience becomes part of our history.

Fellowship is another possible translation of this word. Fellowship describes a present energy, a dynamic that takes place as persons of like mind come together. You cannot have fellowship with a book, or a lecture!

Partnership is a bond between people who are present with you, working together toward a common goal. We cannot enter into a partnership with someone who died last year!

We cannot participate in, have fellowship with, or enter into a partnership with a memory or an aid to memory! These are words that belong to the activity of living persons united in achieving a shared purpose.

In the Eucharist, we meet with the living Christ—His body and blood given to us—and we, with Him, participate, fellowship, share in, and realize our partnership with Him in His resurrected body and His triumphant blood that still speaks the good news! Through the Spirit, Jesus the Son teaches us to participate in fellowship with the Father as He knows Him—as a child knows the Father. Throughout His ministry, Jesus urged people to become as little children to know and experience the kingdom of God. With this comes not only rest but the element of play. Play has no 'have to' attached but is spontaneous, reveling in the moment, catching the winds of joy in our sails! Work stops all of that with its demands: "You have to, must, ought, should and if not ..."

In this Eucharist, we discover that we are truly and inseparably one with Christ and ask Him to open your eyes to learn freedom in life with the Father—with Abba, Dad! Religion has taught us to be afraid of the Father, A pastor once reported that his sermons on the holiness and sovereignty of God terrified his baby girl. He told her that was good, that this was how we should think of Him!

The blessing of the death-destroying body and the covenant cup of His blood is with us wherever and whenever we eat and drink. This is the eternal feast, consumed in time and space, bringing every blessing in the living Christ into this moment.

The expression 'drink this cup' means to make part of your experience, to participate in the contents and substance of the cup. Earlier, we saw Jesus, looking into the fourth cup, draw back in horror as He saw His shed blood and all that was involved in its shedding. Previously, He had given us the third cup, telling us it was His blood shed for us. When He must drink the violence, cruelty, and took upon Himself our sin—His shed blood—He experienced the agony, sweating drops of blood. When we drink the same shed blood, we experience the cleansing, acceptance, no condemnation, inseparable union with Him, and joy and peace beyond all comprehension. Yet we both drank the same blood! As we drink His blood, we contemplate the wonder and the mystery, consuming it with joy unspeakable and full of glory, knowing that He participated in the horror so that we might participate in the wonder! We see Him experiencing the full pain and mental agony as He contemplated drinking, while we contemplate that same blood and are caught up in joy and unearthly peace, celebrating our gift of righteousness.

There is an alternative translation: *'Christ's blood'* could be translated as *'the anointing with His blood.'* This echoes the Old Testament practice where the blood of a sacrificed animal was placed on parts of the body—an anointing with blood. At other times, *the blood was sprinkled* on the person or even a gathered multitude. These expressions carry the same message: that we, the worshiping believers, are not merely viewing this as something done *for us* at a distance but as something *applied directly to us*, the individual.

When the individual was anointed with blood, they were also anointed with sacred oil, symbolizing the Holy Spirit. This foreshadowed the New Testament, where, after the shedding of Christ's blood, we are personally united to all the effects of that blood through the Spirit.

Put this all together, and we find ourselves partaking of the meal of mystery and wonder! We, you and I, eat and drink the body and blood of Christ, and the Holy Spirit applies the wonder of the body, of the incarnation, and the blood of God—given by God to us—now, not as a distant memory but as something *remembered* and *experienced* in this moment. We are participating in all that is found in the *feast of 'finished and done,'* waiting for us to rejoice and now be glad in it.

Jesus broke the bread and said, 'Take, eat; this is My body which is for you.' The word He used, *take,* describes an *active taking* of something that we know is ours, something we are personally associated with. This word is full of action; the one receiving the gift rises to lay hold of the gift they know is theirs. It is akin to what our children do on Christmas morning!

Come, eat, and drink with that kind of excitement—all you need in this moment is being pressed upon you; rise and take, for all is yours in Christ.

We eat and we drink. We are strengthened with divine strength and revelation is given to us, just as it was on the Emmaus Road: 'He was made known to them in the breaking of bread!'

As we *take into us the body and blood*, the Spirit reveals that *Christ is in us*, we are in Him, and He is in the Father. This is the meal of 'done,' 'finished,' 'is,' 'now.' We never come to this table asking for cleansing, for Him to enter into our hearts, or for His acceptance and intimate love! Instead, we come with songs of thanksgiving, knowing we *are* already cleansed, Christ *does* live in us, and we are the much-loved sons and daughters of the Father who delights in us as we come! As we give thanks, we also ask the Spirit to He open our eyes to see even more clearly.

Eating and drinking means that we consume, unite with, and partake of nutrients and strength of the food, participating in the life of the food. The nutrition, via the blood, goes into every cell in the body, becoming exactly what that cell needs. Ultimately, the food becomes me. He gives Himself to us in bread and wine.

Jesus gave us the gift of the bread and wine to make this known in our total person. He, who became flesh, now comes to us in bread, so that in eating we might know His indwelling—not only in a mystical, invisible, and intangible way but through tangible bread, taken into the mouth and chewed as delicious food at a feast—*He dwelling in us and we in Him.*

His entire person, who died, descended into death, and rose from the dead, is now, through the Spirit, alive in usThis encompasses not only His body but all aspects of humanity, including mind, imagination, desires, emotions, perceptions, and all that we express in any given day. When we eat and drink of His body and blood, we are declaring and celebrating this. We feed on that wonder in our own lives, for us to live is Christ. The Messiah fully dwells in us, corporately and individually—personally.

See how when writing this to the Colossians, Paul comes very close to using Eucharistic language:

> "In Him all the treasures of [divine] wisdom (comprehensive insight into the ways and purposes of God) and [all the riches of spiritual] knowledge and enlightenment are stored up and lie hidden... As you have therefore received Christ, [even] Jesus the Lord, [so] walk (regulate your lives and conduct yourselves) *in union with* and conformity to Him. Have the *roots [of your being] firmly and deeply planted [in Him, fixed and founded in Him*], being continually built up in Him, becoming

increasingly more confirmed and established in the faith, just as you were taught, and abounding and overflowing in it with thanksgiving… For in Him the whole fullness of Deity (the Godhead) continues to dwell in bodily form [giving complete expression of the divine nature]. And you are in Him, *made full and having come to fullness of life [in Christ you too are filled with the Godhead — Father, Son and Holy Spirit — and reach full spiritual stature].*" Colossians 2:3-10 (AMP)

"Christ, because in Him there is continuously and permanently at home all the fullness of absolute deity in bodily fashion. And you are in Him, *having been completely filled full with the present result that you are in a state of fullness.*" Colossians 2:4 (Wuest Expanded Translation)

That's the feeling one gets after a sumptuous meal! We are filled with the Triune God in the ascended Christ. We are called to a meal of wonder, in which the Spirit brings the fullness of God to the specific need we presently experiencing! We eat of the ascended God-Man, of the incarnation—not a doctrine to be studied, but a meal to be joyfully consumed. He speaks of us 'eating my flesh'—not as a map for us to follow, trying to do as He does or go where He goes, and not as an inner influence! The phrase that He used means *to chew His flesh* as one would at the food at a feast—this is the meal of thanksgiving and rejoicing.

We grow in understanding of our having been washed, cleansed within, and our identity as a son or a daughter of God, who can look Him in the face and boldly call Him Abba —the name of intimacy reserved for members of the family. With this assurance, we know that we belong in the Trinity family; in Christ, we are as accepted as He is, delighted in and welcomed by the Father. We drink and know that we have been rescued from the kingdom of darkness; in Christ, Satan is under our feet, for we overcome by the blood of the Lamb and in the word of our testimony at this meal. By the engulfing pain and wounds of the lash, when His blood was shed, we were and are healed; we eat and drink the elixir of resurrection life.

This is the mood of celebration as we eat and drink; as this bread and wine enter our body, so Christ has and does live within us. Every bite, every sip, and we are reveling in all that the body and blood speaks to us of.

2 Peter 1:4 says that we *partake of the divine nature*—the same word as 'participate' is used in Corinthians. This must have been the widespread understanding, as Peter and Paul ministered in different circles.

It brings us again to face what is believed by many to be the condition of unbelievers—that we have a sinful nature in need of getting a divine nature. However, we have human nature, which naturally inclines us, the created, to be in fellowship with the Father in the Son in the Spirit. That is our blueprint from before creation. That is not odd or unusual but expected—our God-given nature.

In Africa, we were warned to stay out of the way of the animals because when they might attack, they are not being 'bad animals!' Tell a lion or hippopotamus that they are bad, and they will simply shrug and say, "It is my nature." Similarly, multitudes of believers will excuse their behavior by saying, *"I have sin nature; it's just the way I am!"* With a sinful nature, even the best of believers can only manage sin and try to be like Jesus.

Our expression 'Christ is my life' means that we partake of His divine nature. Fellowship with the Father in Christ is not odd or strange to us as humans—but natural for our created, redeemed human nature. Anything else leaves us living as less than the humans we are created to be.

So, what do these texts together say? They tell us that we eat and drink of His nature revealed in His body and blood. One might expect such a meal to be lofty, complicated, reserved for spiritual masters! But it is simple: bread and wine, accessible to even the poorest or when everything has been lost.

With our nature being in Christ, one with the Father, we can go and sin no more. Born of God, we are no longer bound to sin, but can put it off like an old, torn, and dirty garment. We can offer our members to the new, now-revealed Christ-nature (Romans 6).

> "And I heard a loud voice from the throne,
> saying, "Behold, the tabernacle of God
> is among men, and He will dwell
> among them, and they shall be His

> people, and God Himself will be
> among them." Revelation 21:3-4

One would expect that it would say that the tabernacle of man is with God! Religion is littered with that idea—reaching up to build a tabernacle, finding a way to dwell with God! But the message of grace is that He has taken the initiative: His Tabernacle has come to us. In the incarnation, God has come down to live with and in us.

Dwell among is better translated as *dwell in them*, fitting with the promises of John 14 that the Trinity will abide with us, and we will abide with Him—that we will bear the family name as we dwell in Him, and He in us.

> This is what we celebrate in every Eucharist: that in Christ, God has come down and dwells with us.

Man, lost in the darkness of the lie, lifts *his* flesh, the sum of *his* abilities, to a God *he has been taught is separated and beyond him*. But the Gospel proclaims that God gave *His flesh* and, on cross, offered *His flesh* and shed *His blood* for us, *as us*, while we remain excluded from adding anything to that by our own efforts.

17. Necessary Meal

But it was necessary to celebrate and to rejoice, because this brother of yours was dead, and is alive, and was lost, and is found! Luke 15:32 (Lexham English Bible)…

Jesus spread a table for a meal and sent out invitations. The meal, suggestive of festivity and feasting, had been the problem from the beginning. Jesus was inviting those whom religion said had no right to be there—the collectors of the Roman taxes, and those who, for whatever infraction of the Law, had been excommunicated from the synagogue. It was a scandal to invite them, and He received and ate with them—a covenant meal. The argument was not that He talked with them, but that he had initiated the feast as a celebration: "Welcome into My family, My society." This was the message that was sent out across the hill country of Galilee and beyond, down into Jerusalem. With curled lips, looks of disgust and loathing, the holy men connected to the synagogue and the Temple, spat out the words, "He receives sinners and eats with them!"

These stories are His response to the religious crowd, explaining the unforgettable worth God places on the human. When one person's eyes are opened and they are saved from certain death, then to feast, to overflow with joy, and to congratulate is a matter of absolute necessity! To be in the atmosphere of such rejoicing is life-changing, penetrating the heart of all present. Apart from such a feast, the saving of the precious human lacks depth and reality—it becomes merely a rumor. The first parables of the chapter—the lost sheep and the lost coin—put all these ideas in one phrase at the end of each story: *"Rejoice with me."* This word, 'rejoice,' sums up the meal as one of joy, singing, and dancing. The final story we find in this chapter—the entire story—is built around a feast that involves the entire village.

What did it mean? The younger brother had come home from a life that had fallen apart in the far country of the Gentiles. To the religious ears, that meant he had drunk deeply of all the sins of the Gentiles and had spent his father's Jewish money in Gentile stores and houses of entertainment. They shrugged their shoulders, bent heavy with their piety, unlike them, such a person was to be thrown aside and made to pay for his sin—forever.

In this story, told by Jesus, the Master storyteller, the younger son, starving to death in the far country, came home to try to make things right with his father—if for nothing else, to get a decent meal. He comes with a confession of sin, self-loathing, and suggested penance all memorized, ready to spill it out when he meets his father. It was a perfect confession—good enough to make a Pharisee dance in his grave! But instead, the father showed complete disinterest in such matters. He interrupted the boy's confession of sin as he groveled in the muck of unworthiness, hugging the young man's filthy body and reeking clothes, calling him "My son!" He dismissed the past as done and gone—"*was lost,* is found, *was dead,* and is alive"—a past buried in the rejoicing, forgiveness, and joy lavished upon the returned son.

Anticipating such a day, the father had fattened up a young bull, and it was now turning on the spit. The smell of roasting beef was the call to the village for the feast of feasts!

The son had returned, afraid of whether he would be welcomed or rejected. He was met with love beyond any definition he had known—sin dismissed, kindness, clothed in apparel to look like the son he was, his father's son—even though, at that moment, he was asking to be made a hired slave. He was met with grace; he contributed not one behavior. His promises of reformation were canceled even as he was trying to put them into words. The entire event radiated from his father, who initiated the forgiveness, the hugs that would not stop, and the kisses all over that filthy body. It was the father who called for the servants to begin serving the dazed son—a bath (for sure), another dismissed to the house to bring the father's best robe, his party robe, and shoes for the son's feet, which had not seen shoes in months. And again, it was the father who took one skinny hand and slipped a signet ring on the finger—the family covenant ring. It declared to all who saw him that he was truly a son in his father's family.

That day, he got to know his father, meeting him for the first time! All those years of living in his father's house, obsessed with himself, he had never known his father—only a caricature that was passed through the lens, reinterpreted according to his and his elder brother's preconceived notions. Now, savoring a love never known before, he responded with love to the love that his father lavished on him. He submitted to what made no sense—the event of forgiveness—and then to the feast held in his honor, for the entire town to welcome him home. Those who could not fit in the house spilled over onto the lawns and grassland, Music began, and dancing in circles of joy, the villagers joined in the father's welcome.

The only stranger to the wild joy in the village was his older brother, who had been working in the fields or watching others' work to the crack of his whip! The faint sounds of instruments, laughter, shouts of gladness and joy, and the distinct smell of roast beef disturbed his reverie as he strode across the field toward home. Anything happening on the ranch without his knowledge or permission made him uneasy, and that uneasiness was quickly turning to anger. As he came to the edge of town, he saw a servant taking a break from the party, and the older brother accosted him, demanding to know the reason for the feast. The servant, fearful of the man who was his boss and now leaned menacingly into his face, told him that his brother had come home. The father had received him with peace, health and safety (he would have said "Shalom"), and now the entire village was dancing for joy in the honor of his brother!

Rage that had simmered just below the surface now exploded. It was bad enough that his father had lost his mind in welcoming that worthless, shameful man back home, but the age-old custom established throughout Israel was that, at such a time, the elder son, must take the father's place as master of ceremonies—making sure everyone is seated, fed, and attended to—while the father, free of pressure, visited with the honored guest. He, the elder brother, was expected to hover, serving the honored guest above all others. He shuddered with rage and horror at the thought of giving premium service to the one who had brought only embarrassment and shame to the family, especially to him. The world had gone mad! He couldn't be associated with such insanity! In his mind, he had already divorced himself from them all—especially his crazy father! In a few minutes, he would speak to the father and tell him that the younger sibling was "your son," not "my brother"!

He came toward the house, where the servants on the porch were impatiently waiting for him. They were poised to ready him to enter the party and take his place as Head Waiter and Master of the Feast. He would then be expected to assume his special assignment to the honored guest—his brother—and fulfill his every need and pleasure. The servants had the door ready to open when the oldest son's rage spilled over the porch and could be heard in the main dining room. He did not, and never would, go into the festivities! His father could look after the party he had called for… as for his brother, he was not welcome here and could go back to his Gentile friends faster than he had left them.

His rage blinded him to the consequences of his action. He had shamed his father, which was the unspeakable sin in the Jewish household. The punishment, rooted in the book of Proverbs, was strictly enforced so that the eldest son of every family in town would think twice before losing control. Every large property had a simple jail, and if the parents were so shamed, the servants would be sent at once to arrest the foolish man and throw him in the jail, waiting for his father's rage to cool before punishment. Beatings with rods would leave the rebellious man in pain he would never forget.

The guests waited for the protocol to unfold, as it had for a thousand generations. The father would be shamed and enraged by the antics of the son, who stood on the porch at the doorway. He would then call a servant to arrest the rebellious son, who would be taken away to the on-property jail. The feast would resume as if nothing had happened, and the father's honor and authority would be securely restored. But on this night, nothing of the kind happened. The embarrassed silence was interrupted only by the shouts of the oldest son, resisting the servants who were trying to get him into the feast as quickly as possible. Then the father rose to his feet, walked to the door, and without looking back, stepped onto the porch, leaving everyone staring at each other, whispering loudly, "What is he doing?"

The father was involving himself, sharing the shame of his son. Out on the porch, in the darkness of the night, where the servants stood waiting to be summoned to take their place in the feast, the son turned in amazement seeing that his father had joined him there. The father came alongside the son and began to speak gently, confusing everyone even more. If the old man was going to take the arrest out of the hands of the servants, he was supposed to do it with a rage at least equal to that of the son!

Let us pick up the story directly from the mouth of Jesus…

> "But he (the Elder brother) became angry and was not willing to go in; and his father came out and began pleading with him. But he answered and said to his father, "Look! For so many years I have been serving you and I have never neglected a command of yours; and

> yet you have never given me a young goat, so that I might celebrate with my friends; but when this son of yours came, who has devoured your wealth with prostitutes, you killed the fattened calf for him." And he (the father) said to him, 'Son, you have always been with me, and all that is mine is yours. But we had to celebrate and rejoice, for this brother of yours was dead and has begun to live and was lost and has been found.'" Luke 15:28-32

The attitude of the elder son is that of an overlooked slave. In his speech to his father, he gives no indication that he is this man's son! He does not address the man beside him as 'father,' but rather as the slave master! He plunges right in, giving himself accolades, as if declaring himself the slave of the month: "Look! For so many years I have been serving you, and I have never neglected a command of yours…" The literal translation is, "… I have been a slave to you." All the discussions between father and son about the goals of the ranch had been interpreted by the son as meetings in the boss's office to receive another list of tasks that must be done to keep his job.

The father stood beside him on the porch. Jesus uses a very different word now than the one He used back in the field, where the elder son asked the passing servant what was going on. At that time, the word describes a threatening stance—'in your face,' demeaning the listener. Now, the word used to describe the father coming to the son on the porch means to *come alongside*, to gently lead without bullying. The Greek word is the same one Jesus used to describe the Holy Spirit, *paraclete,* coming alongside to strengthen and gently direct, translated here as 'pleading.'

With his slave mentality, the elder son had waited to be singled out and rewarded for his perfect record! Month after month, he waited, but no reward was forthcoming—not even a baby goat to BBQ with his friends. Sadly, he was not looking for quality time with his father, but rather time away from the ranch to party with his friends. He shames his younger brother, accusing him of squandering his inheritance on prostitutes and immoral living.

The father's response is the truth cutting to the heart of the problem…

> "And he (the father) said to him, 'Son, you have always been with me, and all that is mine is yours.'"

The word Jesus used to address him is of great importance. The Hebrews had specific words to describe each stage of growing up. Sometimes these words overlap if the person speaking is simply identifying a child as belonging to them. But here, Jesus, the storyteller, is very deliberate in choosing His words to identify the two brothers. The word used for a teenager—biologically the child of the parent, but acting like a teenager, not yet a full-grown, mature son able to represent the father or the family—is *teknon.* The word *huios* describes a full-grown, mature son, capable of representing the father and the goals of the present family, as well as the family's goals revealed through previous generations, stretching back hundreds of years.

When the inheritance was divided at the beginning of the story, the eldest son, according to the law of Deuteronomy, would have received two-thirds of the inheritance, while the younger received only a third. Why? So that the elder son, who would eventually take the place of the father and care for the ranch and the family, would have the extra resources to be able to do so. If one family member went astray, as the younger son had, the elder—now the patriarch—would use the extra cash to pursue, find, and rescue him if necessary, and restore him. But this elder brother, meant to be the kinsman-redeemer, clearly did not care what happened to his younger brother, nor did he use the resources for his brother's rescue. We do not know what he did with the extra cash, but he certainly did not use it to bring his younger brother home, even though he seems to have known where his brother was and what he was doing!

After listening to the self-pitying anger of the older brother, Jesus called him *teknon*—a teenager absorbed with himself, full of self-pity, irresponsible, and lacking understanding of the father or his goals for the immediate family, as well as the intentions of the family through past generations! The elder brother was older biologically and held a position in the family hierarchy, but he was immature in understanding and responsibility. The deliberate use of *teknon* would not be lost on any of the listeners. Especially when, with equal deliberateness, Jesus referred to the younger brother—fresh from his time of destitution in the far country—as *huios*—a full-grown, mature son, ready to take his father's place both in the present moment and in the unfolding history of the family!

Why does the father portray the difference between the two sons? The younger son had experienced *metanoia*—a Greek word that has been translated for centuries as 'repentance,' and is so translated throughout this chapter. But let us be clear: *repentance* in no way represents the true meaning of the Greek word *metanoia*.

The mistranslation of *metanoia* as 'repentance' has defined the Gospel in terms of self-effort, imposing a behavior that would suggest life-change rather than trusting in the action of the Triune God working *for us, as us,* and *in us.* The word *repentance* comes from Latin: *re* meaning 'repeat' or ' do something over and over,' and *pentance*, from *penance*—an act that confirms a forgiveness granted by the church, making us acceptable to God by doing something demanded by the church to earn salvation. This word is so far removed from the truth of the Gospel, that, in our fellowship in Bandera, Tx, we do not use the word 'repentance' at all. Instead, we simply use the Greek word without translating it.

Metanoia means radical enlightenment given by the Holy Spirit, occurring through the proclamation of the truth of the Gospel. It describes flooding the inner person with light, revealing all things as they truly are. With the accompanying power of the Holy Spirit the one enlightened is enabled to stand in and with the truth against the darkness of lies that will inevitably oppose them. *Metanoia* is a moment in which, in a blaze of divine light, we receive a radical change of mind—a reorientation and fundamental transformation of outlook. It changes a person's vision of the world and of themselves, bringing a new way of loving God and others. In the light, we see that this faith is from Him, who is already within us!

The younger son had returned home with a prayer of confession, suggesting his own penance and the place he should take as a failed and worthless sinner. The father, however, cut short this sinner's prayer, engulfing the young man in his arms and bestowing upon him forgiveness and restoration to the family, as his son. In that embrace, the younger son tasted the love of his father and experienced his grace, revealing the father's heart in a way the son had never known before. With his face buried in his father's robe, he heard his father declare: "You are my son. You were lost but now you are found; you were dead but now you are alive again—the past is canceled and swallowed in my love."

In that light, which shone into every crevice of his being, all he had ever thought he knew of his father collapsed in the presence of the Light, and it was replaced with the truth of who his father truly was—and, with it, the truth of who he himself was. He received a new identity! In knowing his father, he came to know himself! He had been a wild, self-absorbed, irresponsible *teknon*, but in that *metanoia* of his father, he began the life journey as *huios*.

The father reminded the whining, self-pitying man beside him on the porch, "Son, (*teknon*) you have always been with me, and all that is mine is yours." The father had taken all that was his and divided it between the two sons. When the younger left for the far country, turning his inheritance into cash, it left the elder brother owning everything the father possessed. The father was essentially saying to the eldest son, "You whine because I don't pay you, reward you with bonuses, or give you animals to BBQ, but you have forgotten—*I have already given you everything I have. I have chosen not to have anything that I cannot make yours!* You could BBQ every animal on the ranch if you wanted – they are all yours! You could set your own salary; all the money is yours! But wallowing in your slave identity keeps you from seeing yourself as anything more than a beggar!

And I am everything that you are searching for, a relationship with me would fill the emptiness of your restless heart—you haven't noticed, but I have never left you. I have been with you in every moment, just as I am right now."

How can this boy become a *huios*? How can he enter a world of light where he clearly sees the truth? How can he find forgiveness for himself and his brother? How will he come to know his father and receive his embrace? How will he come alive from the dead as his brother had? We wait, looking to the father—what will he say that can bring this wretched, religious Pharisee to know God, himself, and his world?

> "But we had to celebrate and rejoice, for this brother of yours was dead and has begun to live and was lost and has been found. Come, tread the pathway everyone in the village has taken, including your brother. It is the only way!"

"We had to celebrate…" The word translated 'had to' is better understood as 'necessary, we are bound, the only possible action under the circumstances; needful; necessity.' This word appears several times in the New Testament to describe divine necessity—Jesus said His sufferings and death at the hands of wicked men was a 'had to,' a necessity, the only way He could go.

> I am stunned! This miserable man, with a selfish teenage mind, is to be rescued from himself to walk the path to *huios*—by going through that door to a party!! There is divine action in that party!

To enter through that door means you will be plunged into the divine energies of God-love, into grace upon grace, into rest as you come to know the father for the first time. You will discover your brother, serve him, and experience both dying and rising again! It is necessary you join us, come, eat and drink, receive love, and rest in the truth your eyes have not seen and your ears have not heard.

Your pathway to being and growing in Christ is not endless Bible studies and acts of dedication, but through the Meal of Wonder and Mystery that invites you to turn the latch and step into a new world! This is the reality of the wardrobe that was a door to Narnia! It is the rabbit hole of *Alice in wonderland!* A simple meal that is necessary to our growth in Christ, within the Father's Family.

As we finish this chapter, let us turn to the response we make to this Gospel, which comes to us through His body and blood. You come before the celebrant, who holds the body of Christ in his hands and says, "This is the body of Christ, the bread of heaven," and the one receiving responds joyfully, "Amen!"

Amen—the most ancient way of saying "I believe"—it is far stronger than the casual way people mean it today when they say they believe! The word means: an expression of strong agreement, "It is so," "So be it," "That is the way it is," "Final reality," "Certainty"—an emphatic assent.

It was spoken to declare the ratification of a covenant or a solemn oath. It is our response to the words of God, who has declared, "Jesus Christ is our salvation; He is our eternal life; in Him it is done, accomplished, and finished," and we respond with great joy and gladness, "Amen!" We do not argue with His Word; His words are non-negotiable. We do not present an alternate plan—it is not something we vote on— it is the way it is: immoveable, unchangeable, unshakeable.

Upon this, we rest our exhausted bodies, our confused minds, our ragged emotions, our searching, longing spirits—our total and essential selves—free-falling into His divine peace. As we say *Amen*, we receive all that is ours because now we see differently, no longer through the lens of "What must I do? What is my penance?" but through "What has He done? Open my eyes to see all that is already mine!"

Christ has died, Christ is risen, Christ is ascended for and as me—and that is the way it is! On this, I build my life!

Note From the Author

I meet every Thursday morning with our staff, specifically with those we count as "my sons and daughter in Christ" These individuals have been with me for years, and I have given myself to them. Over the last year, as I've been indisposed, they've taken my place, and under their preaching and pastoring, our congregation has grown!

A few months ago I shared with them that I felt our Eucharist celebration did not fully express what we had come to understand about the finished work of Christ and our place in Him today. I suggested that over the next weeks or even months, they could submit any parts that they felt could be updated, along with their ideas.

The following week, Andrew came in having rewritten the entire service—obviously led by the Spirit. There were tears of joy, and we immediately celebrated the Eucharist using what Andrew had put together, and as we did, the Spirit bore witness. I asked Andrew to write a few notes on what he had done, and I am including a copy of the Eucharist service that we now use every Sunday in our fellowship in Bandera and on Zoom.

Malcolm Smith

Eucharist: Meal of Wonder by Andrew S. Coloney

"This is the same body that was covered in blood, pierced by the spear, pouring forth the saving streams of blood and water for the whole world. Christ soared up from the abyss in dazzling light and leaving his rays there he went up to his throne in heaven. It is that body that he gives us to hold and eat now."

JOHN CHRYSOSTOM

"A few drops of blood redeem the whole universe"

GREGORY NAZIANZEN

All throughout Scripture, God retells the story of His working in the lives of the people with whom He enters into covenant; "I am the God who took you out of Egypt." Entering into covenant demands the retelling of joined histories and what covenant faithfulness will look like in the unfolding relationship of union. At the Eucharist Service, we give thanks to the Father for the Son in the Holy Spirit, in a retelling of His covenant faithfulness—not just as history, but in an antiphonal celebration of the real and present body and blood of the now resurrected, ascended, glorified, and death-destroying Lord Jesus Christ, who feeds us with His very own life.

When Bishop Malcolm asked our Thursday morning group to start thinking about how we could update our Eucharist service to better reflect our Fellowship's revelation and understanding of the work of the Holy Trinity in redemptive history, my heart leaped at the opportunity! I went home that afternoon, sat on my bed with a copy of *Eucharist Rite II Prayer D* from the *Book of Common Prayer*—which we were using at that time for our Eucharist—and I began the process of laying out, in no uncertain terms, a history of The Father, Son and Holy Spirit's covenant faithfulness.

I want to focus on three main sections of our Eucharistic Liturgy. These were restated to reflect the revelation that the heart of the New Covenant was already present within the fall, unfolding through the Incarnation, and culminating in the pouring out of the Holy Spirit at Pentecost. Just prior to announcing God's faithfulness from within the Fall, it is stated that the Father is "endlessly and unalterably for us." This powerful statement proclaims that the Fall did not *necessitate* the Incarnation. The Incarnation is the natural result of His being for us, and nothing—not sin, not the Fall, not even our rejection of Him—would alter or end His purpose of bringing the fellowship of face to face holy love of the Trinity inside the human race, making us the living temple out of which rivers of living water would flow to cover the Earth.

In the section concerning what happened at the Fall, it is described as the human race being "plunged into the darkness of the lie." From that darkness, we believed God was not for us and too holy to look at us. The Lie put the face of the accuser on the God who, in love, created us to fellowship with Him. This idea of God being too holy to look at sin comes from an incomplete reading of Habakkuk 1:13. Habakkuk says God can not look with favor upon wickedness, but then continues—where most preachers do not: *Why do you look with favor?* Because God is love, and His holiness is His love. And because God is unalterably for us, the issue is not that God is too holy to look at sin; rather, He is too holy to ever look away!

So in believing from within the darkness of the Lie that God was too holy to look at sin, and therefore too holy to look at us—more concerned with a law being kept than our eyes opened to His Fatherly affections, the God who is Love, Father Son and Holy Spirit, shines light out from the darkness. By never turning from us, He once and for all contradicts the Lie. He stands with us against the accuser's lies and promises the crushing of the liar's head through the seed of the woman. This refusal to abandon us to destruction is the wrath of God. It is the shout of Love's *"NO!"* that reverberates throughout the cosmos like a shock wave from a nuclear blast. This is love's response from the God who cannot change.

In the next section, it is stated that Jesus is the Savior who doesn't save us *from* God, but instead takes us to Him! The "good news" of religion begins in the darkness, with the belief that God is not for us and cannot look at us. In this view, the gospel is then seen as Jesus being the ultimate fig leaf that perfectly hides us from the Father, saving us *from* Him. Adam was right to hide from such a holy god—he just didn't have a fig leaf big enough. But the gospel of light shines forth from under that fig leaf, revealing that the justice of God being satisfied means we are brought home, face to face with the Father in the Son, to know as we have always been known.

This purpose of the Trinity, unaltered by sin, finds its pathway of fulfillment even into our death. But, by His life, He destroys death, takes the keys to hell and the grave, and raises humanity to be seated in heavenly places. In Luke 4, Jesus quotes from Isaiah, declaring that He has come to set the captives free and announces Jubilee—the restoration of all things to their rightful owner. In Revelation 1, Jesus says that He has the keys to hell and death, and when Jesus holds the keys, He doesn't go around locking people up—He sets them free! In Ephesians, Paul tells us that where Jesus is seated after the ascension, we are seated with Him.

All of this finished work is to then be revealed by the Holy Spirit, who will lead us into all truth. In the final section, which we will examine next, it describes the coming of the Spirit and His purpose.

"And exposing the lie that we were unworthy servants under the gaze of Your disapproval, You sent the promised Holy Spirit—the Blessing of Abraham, the very Spirit of Adoption—who continually intercedes for us, convincing us that we truly are your beloved children, by whom we cry 'Abba, Daddy.'" Jesus is the Seed promised to Abraham and through that Seed, ALL families of the earth would be blessed. Galatians 3 tells us that the Blessing of Abraham is the Holy Spirit. It is so vitally important to remember that the Holy Spirit is the Spirit of Adoption—not Western concept of adoption, where someone is placed in a family to which they have no DNA connection, they wouldn't find them on their "23andMe." In that case, a legal declaration makes one a part of a family they weren't born into. But *adoption* in Scripture speaks of being placed in the family where we actually *do* belong—we truly have the DNA of God. God is all about family! All families of the Earth are blessed by being joined to the original family through the Spirit of Adoption.

Our confession is that we are sons, not unworthy servants. In Luke 15, the prodigal son prepared a letter to explain to his father that he was not worthy to be a son—maybe, just maybe, he might have enough worth to be a servant. But if he wasn't even worthy to be a servant, perhaps there could be a compromise where he would be known as an unworthy servant. And he would continually thank this man—whom he dare not call "Daddy"—for allowing him to exist by groveling and knowing his place.

This is NOT the gospel, nor our confession, nor is it humility.. It's the most arrogant and prideful way to tell God He must deal with us on *our* terms. YOU ARE MY SON! This is the confession of the Father, and this is our confession in our Eucharist Liturgy. The Lie says, "grovel," but He who is Truth said, "Arise!." We don't say "Master"—we say "Daddy"!

In the Eucharist, we give thanks from the revelation of truth and retell the story of God's covenant faithfulness. This Truth is the ultimate scandal to both religion and to the world. The God who is almighty love—the Father, the Son and the Holy Spirit—treasures our fellowship and our inclusion in that love above all else. But it is not just a retelling of history; it is New Covenant remembrance, something only the Holy Spirit can accomplish—bringing an event from the past into the present now, making it manifest in our time and space with all its accompanying consequences, ramifications and results.

At the Cross, I believe there was a nuclear explosion in the spirit world that sent shock waves throughout the entire cosmos. Just as the 6,000 men in the Garden of Gethsemane were laid flat on their backs at the very mention of the Name of God, so too were every principality and power of darkness laid flat as this shock wave destroyed their kingdom. If words mean anything, then every time the Eucharist is celebrated anywhere in the world, the remembrance brought by the Holy Spirit sends the same devastating shock wave throughout the cosmos, tormenting all the powers of darkness. Like the toll of a bell piercing the night air, it resounds with the sound of their doom: "Christ is Risen! Christ is Risen! Christ is Risen!"

So, after updating the language of our Eucharist Liturgy to better reflect our theology, I believe we have come into harmony with the conclusion of Irenaus when he stated "Our teaching is in harmony with the Eucharist, and the Eucharist confirms our teaching." Every Sunday, in a small stone chapel in Bandera Texas, our little fellowship comes together, giving thanks to the Father, for His Son in the Holy Spirit. Then, we participate in the greatest mystery of mysteries and wonder of wonders: we eat the flesh and drink the blood of the One in, for, and through whom all things were created—He is before all things, in whom all things hold together, and in whom all the fullness of the Godhead—Father, Son and Holy Spirit—dwells in bodily form.

He who fills the cosmos, yet cannot be contained by it, meets us there, in that tiny little chapel, to be received in our hands and sipped from a chalice. Who is like unto Thee among the gods?

Unconditional Love Fellowship Eucharist Service

CELEBRANT: The Lord be with you. **PEOPLE: "AND ALSO WITH YOU"**

CELEBRANT: Lift up your hearts. **PEOPLE: "WE LIFT THEM TO THE LORD"**

CELEBRANT: Let us give thanks to the Lord our God. **PEOPLE: "IT IS RIGHT TO GIVE HIM THANKS AND PRAISE"**

It is truly right to glorify You, Father, and to give You thanks. For You are face to face with the Son in the Spirit, Eternal Life, dwelling together in the divine dance of holy unity, from before time and forever. Fountain of Life, source of all goodness, You made all things in the Son, and in Him all things hold together and are filled with Your blessing. You created them to rejoice in the splendor and brilliance of Your kind intention. Countless throngs of angels stand before You to serve You night and day, joining with them, as a Kingdom of Priests, representing and giving voice on behalf of all creation, we acclaim You and glorify Your name as we say:

CELEBRANT AND PEOPLE: "TO HIM WHO SITS ON THE THRONE AND TO THE LAMB BE BLESSING AND HONOR AND GLORY AND DOMINION FOREVER AND EVER"

We acclaim You Holy Lord, The Three in One, glorious in love. Your goodness and kindness reveal that You are endlessly and unalterably for us. You formed us in Your own image, giving the whole world into our care, so that in fellowship with You, our Father, we might rule and serve all Your creatures.

When we were plunged into the darkness of the lie, believing that You were not for us, too holy to look at us, You contradicted the lie, never turning from us, and took sides with us against the accuser, promising the crushing of his head by the woman's seed. In Your wrath, the passionate NO! of Your love that refused our abandonment and destruction, You came into our darkness to seek us until You found us.

Father, You loved the world so much that in the fullness of time, You sent Your only Son, to be our Savior; not to save us from You, but to take us to You. Incarnate by the Holy Spirit, born of the Virgin Mary, He lived as one of us yet without sin. To the poor He proclaimed the Good News of Salvation, to prisoners, freedom, and to the sorrowful, joy. And to fulfill Your purpose, He gave Himself up to death, and rising from the grave destroyed death, taking with Him the keys to hell and the grave, raising humanity to be seated in heavenly places, making the whole creation new.

And exposing the lie that we were unworthy servants under the gaze of Your disapproval, You sent The Promised Holy Spirit, The Blessing of Abraham, The Spirit of Adoption, Who continually intercedes for us, convincing us that we truly are Your beloved children, by whom we cry "Abba, Daddy".

When the hour came for Him to be glorified by You, His heavenly Father, having loved His own who were in the world, He loved them to the end.

At supper with them He took bread. And when He had given thanks to You, He broke it, and gave it to His disciples and said "Take eat, this is My body, which is given for you. Do this for the remembrance of Me."

After supper He took the cup. And when He had given thanks to You, He gave it to them and said, "Drink this, all of you, this is My blood of the New Covenant, which is shed for you and for many, for the undoing of sin, whenever you drink it, do this for the remembrance of Me."

Father, we now celebrate this memorial of our redemption. Recalling Christ's death and descent among the dead. Proclaiming His resurrection and ascension to your right hand, and announcing our sharing in glory: We in Him, He in us, and together in You. And offering to You the gifts You have given us, this Bread and this Cup, we praise You and we bless You:

CELEBRANT AND PEOPLE: "WE PRAISE YOU, WE BLESS YOU, WE GIVE THANKS TO YOU, AND WE PRAY TO YOU LORD OUR GOD"

Lord we thank you that The Holy Spirit, who brings all things to our remembrance and reveals that we are partakers of The

Divine Nature, now descends upon these gifts, showing them to be Holy Gifts for Your Holy People. The Bread of Life, the Cup of Salvation, the Body and Blood of Your Son, our savior, Jesus Christ.

Grant that all who share this bread and this cup, are shown to be one body and one spirit, a living sacrifice in Christ, to the praise of Your Name.

Remember, Lord, Your One, Holy, Universal and Apostolic Church, redeemed by the blood of Your Christ. Reveal our unity, guard our faith and preserve us in Your peace.

And grant that we may find our inheritance with patriarchs, prophets, apostles, and martyrs and all Saints who have found favor with You in all times and places. We praise You in union with them and give You glory through Your Son Jesus Christ our Lord.

CELEBRANT AND PEOPLE: "THROUGH CHRIST AND WITH CHRIST AND IN CHRIST ALL HONOR AND GLORY ARE YOURS, ALMIGHTY GOD AND FATHER, IN THE UNITY OF THE HOLY SPIRIT, FOREVER AND EVER, AMEN."

THE LORD'S PRAYER

CELEBRANT: Hallelujah! Christ our Passover is sacrificed for us.

CELEBRANT AND PEOPLE: THEREFORE, LET US KEEP THE FEAST! HALLELUJAH! HALLELUJAH! AMEN.

CELEBRANT: The Gifts of God for the people of God. Take them in remembrance that Christ died for you by dying as you. And now feed on Him, this His resurrected, ascended, glorified, death-destroying body and do so in your hearts with thanksgiving!

(The Bread and the Cup are given to the communicants with these words)

CELEBRANT: The Body of Christ, the Bread of Heaven. **PEOPLE: "AMEN"**

CELEBRANT: The Blood of Christ, the Cup of your Salvation. **PEOPLE: "AMEN"**

CELEBRANT AND PEOPLE: ALMIGHTY AND EVER-LIVING GOD, WE THANK YOU FOR FEEDING US WITH THE SPIRITUAL FOOD OF THE MOST PRECIOUS BODY AND BLOOD OF YOUR SON, OUR SAVIOR, JESUS CHRIST. AND FOR ASSURING US IN THESE HOLY MYSTERIES THAT WE ARE LIVING MEMBERS OF THE BODY OF YOUR SON AND HEIRS OF YOUR ETERNAL KINGDOM. AND NOW FATHER, SEND US OUT, TO DO THE WORK YOU HAVE GIVEN US TO DO, TO LOVE AND SERVE YOU AS FAITHFUL WITNESSES OF CHRIST OUR LORD. TO HIM, TO YOU AND TO THE HOLY SPIRIT BE HONOR AND GLORY, NOW AND FOREVER, AMEN.

THE BLESSING

CELEBRANT: Let us go forth into the world, rejoicing in the power of the Spirit.

CELEBRANT AND PEOPLE: THANKS BE TO GOD! HALLELUJAH! HALLELUJAH! AMEN!"

About the Author

Malcolm Smith was born in London, England, immediately before World War II he came to a personal knowledge of the Lord Jesus in his early teens. He experienced the infilling of the Holy Spirit that changed his life forever. From the very beginning of his life in Christ, he was 'arrested' by 1 John 4, "God is Love." He not only has love —but IS LOVE! The Holy Spirit fueled a passion for knowing HIS love in its fullness.

Malcolm has pursued that desire for the past 70-plus years. He began teaching in his early teens and was pastor of churches in London and Ireland before coming to the U.S. in 1964. While pastoring a church in Brooklyn, N.Y., he encountered the Holy Spirit that plunged him into the emerging Charismatic movement that opened all denominations to his message. Since then, he has traveled worldwide, teaching believers who they are in Christ.

He presently lives in Bandera, Tx. with his wife, Cheryl, who brings with her many years of ministry experience in women's prisons, having served as women's staff chaplain of Harris County Jail from '92-2002. They conduct retreats and bible schools and minister to a weekly fellowship on Sunday mornings in Bandera on the ministry ranch.

He has hundreds of hours of teaching on CD and mp3 and hundreds of video hours on YouTube at Malcolm Smith webinars.

For further information, find us online at www.unconditionallove-fellowship.com.

He has authored several books, including *The Power of the Blood Covenant* and *This Son of Mine, Expanded Edition, and Toxic Love.*

Made in United States
Troutdale, OR
12/28/2024

27367994R10142